OUR FATHER'S HOUSE

OUR FATHER'S HOUSE

An approach to worship

Bernard Thorogood

THE UNITED REFORMED CHURCH

First published 1983 by
The United Reformed Church
86 Tavistock Place
London WC1H 9RT

GS68 1.2.10.83

© 1983, Bernard Thorogood

ISBN 0-902256-69-6

Typeset by Texet, Leighton Buzzard, Bedfordshire
Made and printed in Great Britain by
Hartnoll Printers Ltd., Bodmin, Cornwall

CONTENTS

Introduction 7

1. Nor dies the strain of praise away 9
   Openers 12

2. Together in Worship 13
   Prayers 19

3. Singing 20
   Prayers 23

4. Playing 25
   Prayers 30

5. Reading 31
   Bible characters 36

6. Expounding 41
   Prayers 47

7. Giving 48
   Dedicatory prayers 53

8. Eating and Drinking 54
   Communion Prayers 60

9. Silence 62

10. Blessing 67
    Benedictions 72

11. Routine or Revelation 73
    Five Senses 77

12. Ecumenical Worship 84
    Prayers 91

13. Shapes, Sizes, Heights and Depths 93
    Prayers 100

14. A Note on 'Given-ness' 102

15. Purposes and Ends 106
    Prayer Moments 116

16. Vision and Reality 121
    What shall I bring? 126

Introduction

I am not a specialist in the history or theology of worship, and I write as one who finds worship at the centre of the Christian life and who is often given the opportunity to lead worship. This is not a formal text from the Church House desk but a personal conversation between fellow pilgrims.

Since I began my ministry in the islands of Polynesia it has been a joy to worship in many countries and many styles. There are major differences between the various traditions, but those who worship in a strange place or a strange communion also find many familiar features. I believe the convergence today is greater than in earlier generations. This is partly due to a wider sharing in the ecumenical movement, partly to the greater freedom within major traditions, and perhaps also to the common life in a secular society which is the experience of all Christians. So although I am thinking of the worship in the church which I serve, much of this little book will be familiar ground to others.

Within the United Reformed Church we have a strong worship tradition. I am very thankful for the rich material we have gathered for our praise and our prayers, and for faithful preaching. Yet it is easy to lose our concentration and accept the pattern of worship as a routine which we believe is good for us but does not stir our hearts. So my concern is to remind myself about what we are doing, so that we may do it with heart and mind and strength.

There is a mixture of material here. Between the chapters I have placed some prayers and meditations. As we read we may also pray, and perhaps others will be encouraged to express freshly their heartaches, hopes and delight in the Lord.

Bernard Thorogood

ONE

Nor dies the strain of praise away

The first impression is of freshness and light. Recently the walls and ceiling were repainted and all the old furniture was taken out, to be replaced with very light wooden chairs with pale green seats and a simple lectern-cum-pulpit and a communion table that is light in colour and reflects light from the windows. It is springtime, full of gold and green. The service begins with chatter, everyone talks with a neighbour and the minister joins in. The whole service must have some planning behind it, yet it seems quite free and informal. There are some modern hymns, with a guitar, and several people read verses from the bible. There is no sermon but a series of comments on various aspects of the theme. Then, all the chairs are moved into small discussion groups for ten minutes before the final hymn, followed by coffee for all.

Here we are impressed by size and height. Those rafters up there must be fifty feet above us. The organ pipes reach up with their pulsing bass. The woodwork glows, polish over dark varnish. Behind the pulpit there is a dark red curtain, and dark red runners cover the pews. What a place to heat with those old-fashioned bulky radiators; it is only really warm on Sunday evening. The worship is familiar. The volume of the organ completely drowns our voices, as though the memory of past crowds and choirs controls those keys and stops. The reading of the bible and the sermon are central. The pulpit is central, the lighting is directed there, the proportion of time given to preaching is dominant and we wait, expectantly, for a word from the Lord. Afterwards we go out down the steps to a dimly lit city street.

Here all is brick. Neat, new and strong, although it was built

9

in the 1930's, there is a well-tended air about it. You feel that the caretaker must also be a handyman who would never tolerate a broken window. Hymn books are stacked precisely in the lobby cupboards and even that tell-tale, the notice board, is neatly covered with current publicity fixed with red drawing pins. There is a crowd on Sunday mornings and still at Christmas and Easter the triumphal song comes true and there are chairs in the aisles. Worship is carefully planned. There is a printed order for everyone. You can follow a progression from adoration and confession to intercession with responsive prayers. The readings follow the lectionary and at communion we use classical prayers. It is a very thoughtful service. If we concentrate and follow carefully we realise what a rich heritage we enter, what a debt we owe to the church of history.

We are in the country and the church is small. There is long grass around the step, a scent of hay from the field and a great bowl of delphiniums in front of the pulpit. The structure is unchanged for a century but the people are very different, far more travelled, educated and varied than they were. The worship has not changed much, being very direct and simple. The old hymns are the favourites. The children's address is appreciated perhaps more than the sermon. It is the conversation after service that seems almost more important, for people are reluctant to leave, there is much to organise and the supply of coffee and biscuits is generous. Outside, children pile into station wagons. There is no resident minister, so any leadership is that which arises within the group, and though this has caused some famous feuds in local history there is today a sense of corporate endeavour.

Just a few of the varied services of worship in our churches. I have had the opportunity to visit many, and a special privilege to add to my memories worship around the world.

Worship on tiny Nassu island or Pukapuka or Rakahanga in the South Pacific, with the simplest white stone building, or a thatched roof, with dogs wandering in and out and a baby being fed and the coconut fronds brushing the windows as the wind blows from the east. Up at Maymyo in the hills of Burma above Mandalay, in a wooden building with hurricane lamps, we spend a wonderful two hours studying the beginning of Mark's gospel, the questions flowing and the interest bubbling over. At Hsin Chu in Taiwan we pray almost in the shadow of the largest statue of Buddha I have seen, with a staircase up inside the concrete arm. Yet the confidence of the prayer is in the power of the risen Christ. In a township outside Bulawayo and another in South Africa, African robed choirs lift hearts and voices so that the gift of harmony becomes a symbol of peace. In Prague there is the sense of a chilly atmosphere outside the great fellowship within the church, with no abbreviated worship but a forty minute sermon on classical lines. And not to be forgotten is the fine wooden tabernacle in New Amsterdam in Guyana where a family of owls had taken up residence in the organ, dive bombing the congregation and quite diverting attention from the sermon.

When we add the whole range of worship with which we are less familiar, the Orthodox and Roman Catholic, the Pentecostal and the house church, the monastic order and the Taize prayers, and recall the variety across the generations, we realise how we are joined to a vast congregation. What we do on Sunday may seem a simple enough routine. Yet it is deep enough, demanding enough, genuine enough to draw the hearts of people in every age and culture. What really are we doing as we worship? Is this an instinct or a fashion? Can we worship in any way that pleases us, or must worship follow a pattern? Does worship change us, or does it only confirm us in our youthful concepts of the faith? Such questions are inevitable as soon as we begin to discuss how we can make a good offering to God that also shares the gospel with the world. We rejoice in the variety of worship, just as we enjoy the variety of people in the Christian family, yet we also believe in a unity of faith. So we look towards the focus of all our worship, that fusion of the heavenly word and the human response, that makes life worship and worship alive.

Jesus Christ is Lord.
At every turn of the road
and on every day of life
we praise him and say,
Jesus Christ is Lord.

Jesus Christ is Lord.
In every language on earth
and in all the songs of heaven
we praise him and say,
Jesus Christ is Lord.

Jesus Christ is Lord.
Through all our fears and doubts
and when we know our sin
we still will praise and say
that Jesus Christ is Lord.

What do we bring to worship? Experiences of God's care,
thoughts about the church, ordinary daily joys and sorrows,
nostalgia, worries about family, a whole store of knowledge,
attitudes to politics, loves, despair, dreams — all we are and
all that our community has given us. We bring all to God.

And God, the creator of life, rejoices in the gift of life and,
in worship, enables us to live more fully in him.

TWO

Together in worship

When you go to church I wonder if you feel that you are doing a strange and complex thing. It is not just a simple matter of attendance with a tick at the end, but there are different levels of meaning and experience. To start with, we are a very mixed bag of people. There is not one identical religious experience repeated in each of us. So different words, emphases, styles come home to different people and we become aware of the many elements in worship which make it comprehensive — or, in the old word, catholic. Perhaps it is a good starting point for worship to look at the company and think about the needs of others. The professor is here and his wife who is losing her sight, the couple from the next road whose son has just survived a motor bike accident, that nice engaged couple, those two old faithfuls who have been church members in the same place for sixty years, the coloured choir member who is the most cheerful ticket collector at the station, and that talkative lad in the juniors — together we come to worship.

For most of us the hour of worship on Sunday morning is the most visible sign that we are Christians. We are stamped as church-goers. Not ear-marked for demotion as in some communist countries and not hunted as in extreme Islamic states, we are still that strange tribe which finds Sunday worship as necessary as the annual holiday. This comes to us from childhood and from conversion. It is a badge of discipleship. Sometimes a chore, sometimes boring, we cannot dismiss that duty of every Christian to join in public prayer and praise. Why is it so central to the Christian life?

We could answer, because participation in the group's public activity is what 'belonging' always means. To be a member of a cricket team and never appear at the ground, to join Rotary but never go to lunch, to be a Scout or Guide but never on parade is to make nonsense of membership. So in Islam the pressure to participate in public prayer is very heavy on the individual; the duty to conform becomes a social cement which upholds stability and the authority of the regime. Not very long ago in Samoa the village elders used to chase delinquents with sticks to chivvy them into church. The relics of that corporate discipline are with us still.

But the argument is not persuasive today in Britain. Unless we are drawn to worship we cannot be pushed. There has to be a correlation between what happens in church and what happens in ourselves, in our personal knowing, feeling, striving, worrying, loving. I suppose there are some occasions when worship is properly a very separated activity; when, for example, the ugliness of daily life is so oppressive that our hearts are drawn towards one hour of beauty. Perhaps part of the attraction of worship in the Soviet Union is this contrast between the drab monotony of the regime and the splendid colour of the sanctuary. Yet escapism is never the whole story. If it were then religion would be a fantasy life resulting in a dangerous split mind and divided heart. The correlation, the continuing reality which is me, a person, a life holds together worship and all other activities. So worship is not restricted to Sunday morning. It is rather an aspect of my whole life of which public worship is the focus.

The links are continuous for us all. Just as we appear at church for baptism, wedding and funeral, so we bring a whole range of human experience to God in worship, we drag with us our disappointments, we lift up our joys, we offer our hopes and secret desires. So we wonder if our worship is compromised as our lives certainly are. We know that we do not put off the garments of selfishness and don a white robe of purity as we pick up the hymn book. The compromises come with us to the house of God and we do not worship with an unmixed adoration. Corporate worship is a fellowship of stumbling pilgrims. When we acknowledge this we are freed from the bland hyprocrisy which has at various times stained all religions. Worship is about life and not about an impossible dream world.

This is one reason why there is always a tension between a formal, traditional pattern and spontaneous, experimental worship. Public worship comes to us as a tradition, we cannot escape that. Two thousand years of practice and of deep thought about what we do in worship have given to us all a body of experience which we would be fools to ignore. Pilgrims who are offered a guide book don't push it aside as of no value. Today we sometimes become impatient of the scholars who have written about the detailed history of the liturgy. We say, 'Why worry where the intercessions come? Why not have half an hour of choruses? Why have a sermon?' I think that we mistake the purpose of liturgical study. It is not an attempt to lay down a law about how we must worship today; rather it is a declaration of how people through the ages have actually been fed spiritually. The guide book tells us where the eating-places are. We are still free to accept their advice or not. Perhaps by not following tradition we shall discover something new, but we may also go hungry.

For the history of worship shows us that a balanced diet is good for spiritual health, and this is assured only if we are careful to follow good models in the design of worship. For example, we may well experiment with an order for Holy Communion which emphasises the community, the sharing with each other, the fellowship and mutual forgiveness. But without the other stress on the coming of God in Christ, the historical event of the cross and the global struggle for the victory of grace, we shall descend to an introverted and sentimental religion. That is not wicked, but neither is it the food we need for a tough journey in a very secularised society.

Yet we also need an element of spontaneity. It is there even in the most strictly ordered worship, for thoughts and images rise in our minds not to order. We value that intimate association between the words of worship and the immediate events of our lives which creates a spark of knowledge — suddenly we see the event in the light of the gospel. There is thus an internal, unobserved activity which is always contemporary with the outward order of worship. 'Let us pray' and, yes, we do; but we cannot ensure a unanimity in the thought processes of the congregation. The pentecostal strain in the Christian community testifies to this. At any point in the worship of the church there may be those unplanned incursions of audible, tangible or visible power which shift the gears, interrupt the flow and point us all towards those spiritual forces which are not to be regulated by a prayer book. Some of us find it hard to rejoice in this. Thrown off balance by the unexpected we may object to individual extroversion demonstrated in church.

This points us towards another abiding tension in worship — it is both individual and corporate and somehow has to keep both in balance. In this country we are very individualist Christians. We tend to regard religion as a private matter between each person and God, almost a secret affair in which eternal destiny depends entirely on subjective faith. If we press that line of thought too far then the life of the church as a body becomes quite unnecessary and the individual understanding or interpretation of faith becomes all-important. This is not the main biblical witness which always places the people of God as a group in the centre of God's saving purpose. Yet, if we then press the corporate nature of worship too hard we shall all have to subscribe to a monastic style in which the words and movements and music are set in one pattern for all to follow. Individuality is lost, sometimes deliberately so, in order that the group may make a single offering of prayer and praise.

In the British context, where individualism constantly tends to isolate us and privatise our religion, it is the corporate nature of worship which needs our attention most. One symbol of this is the imagery of Holy Communion and the non-conformist habit of using little individual glasses. The common cup, dispensed with when thoughts of hygiene were new and demanding, is just one of those vivid symbols of sharing which we need and which — as far as records go — has not increased infections among Anglicans. Another is the giving of the peace, still infrequent in non-conformist worship, in which we actually touch one another, recognise each other as real people and realise that the blessing of peace in Christ is for the here and now, not for some distant spiritual Jerusalem.

This earthing of worship in your life and mine, in our actual experience, is not meant to be destructive of all mystery. During the last twenty-five years we have seen many developments which help to relate worship to daily life, and this is real gain. But we have not found it possible at every point to marry this emphasis with the abiding and over-arching mystery of God's being. Closer to us than breathing, yes, but also and always the unknown, the unexplored, the wholly other and wholly free, the God of Sinai. This note in worship is always important. Because creator and creature are not the same, not to be confused, we know that God speaks within the creation because we have heard his voice in Jesus Christ, but the creation is not God, we are not called to be Pantheists. In worship we move through what is known to the one who makes us wonder and adore.

In describing these tensions in worship we are reminded of its complexity. Simple acts of praise and prayer lead us into the depth of our relationship with each other and with the Maker of heaven and earth. There is, after all, complexity even in the parent-child relationship, however simply that may be expressed. Authority, tradition, love, care, protection, rebellion, growth, confidence, distance — all are part of it and necessary to its fulfilment. This does not interrupt the simplicities of our lives. A laugh shared or a cut bandaged may be simple, spontaneous, unrehearsed and not thought about. It is only with reflection that we see how they were part of a larger pattern of life-long relationship. So in our worship we may praise God simply with a word or a song, with the naïvité of Francis, and no worship could be of higher quality. On reflection we see that each turning to God is part of our pilgrim life, a step in the way of discipleship and therefore not unrelated to our theology; indeed, the worship we offer and the theology we express are two dimensions of one reality, our life in God.

Our loss, our failure is that for so many of us so much of the time worship is boring. That is a reflection on us and not always on the conduct of worship, but it does make us re-examine the style and content of worship. To explain what worship is about, to make the connections with daily life plain, to become more of a community at worship and to keep open the door to all that is spontaneous and expressive of our needs, may be steps to that experience which, from time to time, has lifted us into a new awareness of God.

17

Being together in worship makes us aware of this rich diversity, personal and theological. In the next eight sections we shall look at the individual elements in the normal diet of worship to discern why we do them and how we may give them full meaning and worth.

Worship is so hard for us, Lord. Our minds flit across the surface of life and we find it hard to concentrate. We gather without knowing each other deeply and so our prayers for the fellowship are vague. The world of the bible seems so far away, so hard to understand. So we need your help that our time of worship here may be filled with the joy of your presence. May we know you and your word to us more clearly, may we translate the Bible into our daily lives, may we be joined to the Lord Jesus Christ through our communion and our prayer.

We pray in the Spirit. We cannot pray at all unless the Spirit of God puts it into our hearts to pray. We cannot repent of the wrongs in our past without His judgment of us. Nor can we find a disciple's way through the future unless he guides us into holiness and truth. Heavenly Father, may your Spirit fill us as we worship you.

Father we are a strange gathering of people. We have so many different ideas, so many traditions, such varied relationships. We find it hard to be at one with each other. We even criticise each other. We do not know all the silent pain and sorrow in each other's lives. But you know us altogether. As we worship draw us to the fellowship, give us love and understanding, enable us to act with unity of purpose, and show us the marvellous breadth of your church across space and time.

Everlasting God, you have called us to worship, now enable us to pray and praise with heart and mind, with voice and life so that we may lift up the wonder of your grace made known in Jesus Christ our Lord.

THREE

Singing

Worship and singing belong together in most human cultures. This is very hard for non-musical people. When the chant or the anthem sounds like a squeaking machine, and when you cannot sing a note in tune, it is hard to rejoice in song. Why has this close relation come to pass? It probably has its beginnings in heightened speech. The call to God was not seen by primitive people as a simple chat about the weather to a neighbour. It was a matter of very great moment. It called for dignity and weight. So special words and tones developed with this liturgical significance, and it would seem a slight transition from formalised speech to chanting and from chanting prose to singing verse. Alas for the non-musical! They can only be asked to be patient, for the music will not depart from our worship.

But alas, also, for the very highly musical, the experts in harmony whose ears are offended by hymn tunes below par or congregational singing at the wrong tempo. They also have a hard time in church. They know, technically, how much better the music could be done so it is hard for them to worship through a form that sounds second best. This leads us to think about the place of expertise and perfection and choirs. If the offering of worship to God demands the very highest expression of human artistic ability, if God loves good music and our dedication can best be shown in the quality of our offering, then just as animals for sacrifice needed to be without blemish, so too our music. We shall follow the way of many great traditions and engage the professionals. Who among us can remain unmoved when a fine cathedral choir sings a Bach cantata — perfection of form and execution, texture and line, meaning and melody stirs our hearts to wonder. We are at a sacred concert. And that is precisely the danger we run. We become audience to admire those who perform rather than worshippers engaged in an act of praise.

It is evidently very hard for a church to encourage both the expertise of professionals and the congregational singing of hymns. The balance tends to swing one way or the other with large churches and cathedrals tending to the former and smaller groups to the latter. If the choice has to be made I would follow the congregational way because the first priority is involvement and technical perfection can be only a secondary aim. So I am thankful for the enormous body of competent work in words and music on which we all can draw and in which we can find something to express what is in our hearts. To have a first rate choir as well would be a bonus. It is not difficult to-day for even a small church to have the best choirs, since recordings and amplifiers are so common and excellent. Just a brief period of recorded music may set the tone of a service or highlight a point within it and is not a mechanical intrusion. Where we have skilled organists, choirs and choirmasters their gifts need to be woven into the fabric of the worship, supporting, accenting, enhancing the words of all. 'But that is sheer idealism; you don't know our lot! The same old anthems year after year!' Perhaps we struggle too hard to maintain choirs when we can no longer receive musical leadership from them. There is no liturgical virtue in a choir, provided the congregation becomes its own choir, but there is always virtue in good music.

So how do we help a congregation to sing? It is remarkable, as one travels from church to church, to find such varied traditions of singing, powerful in one place for no apparent reason, feeble in another, youthful in a third. Some stick more or less to old favourites, others are busy writing new hymns and compiling new books. So few generalities apply and each of us makes a personal judgment. Increasingly we seek words which we can sing with integrity, and with understanding.

'We shall sing that magnificent hymn to the Holy Spirit, number 204 in Congregational Praise.' Fine, and we love the Vaughan Williams tune. But what is this all about?

O let it freely burn,
Till earthly passions turn
To dust and ashes, in its heat consuming.

I have often enjoyed this hymn, but still wonder what these words mean. Is the life of the Kingdom bereft of joy and excitement, longing and hope? Are Spirit-filled people the most placid? We move on at the end of the service to 442 and hit the unfortunate lines

> Teach me some melodious measure
> Sung by flaming tongues above,

and wonder whether the tongues above have improved their poetry, despite the flames. It is not only the older hymns which may strike a false note. To me, New Church Praise number 32 is impossible to sing with integrity though it is a recent work — 'God of concrete, God of steel, God of piston and of wheel' seems to me a strange note of praise. Is God responsible for every piston in every internal combustion engine, does he love the piston as he loves you and me? What next?

> God of biro and of watch,
> God of newly bottled Scotch,
> God of armchair and of table,
> God of chutney with green label.

But there is an issue beyond jesting. Modern hymns can readily become so marked a reaction to the flying imagery of the Victorians that they descend to a mundane, trite ordinariness. Between the two extremes there is still a wealth of hymnody which most of us have hardly begun to investigate.

We are fortunate to be living during a period very rich in church music. It comes as a surprise. We are often gloom-laden, budget-burdened, roof-racked congregations, yet among us in Britain there are many songsters, carollers, poets who help us to praise God. Even in the small URC we find there is a stream of new hymns being written and used, some of which are of such quality as to enrich the future church. We seldom look across traditional boundaries to share the songs of others, of Roman Catholics and Lutherans, of black churches, of eastern Europe and other continents. At this point the world church could become a more vivid reality for us all, if we could only open our minds to the different accents in which other parts of the Christian family praise the one Lord.

This applies to words and music. Perhaps it will be the learning from other traditions which will release us from the surprising dominance of the organ to lead our music. When we see older nonconformist churches with the organ pipes as the focal point we may wonder what church architects were at. Did they regard the pipes as somehow holy or meaningful? Or did they simply not know where else to put them? There is perhaps a hint of the bombastic about the growth of organs to dominate the congregation. Earlier, smaller instruments may have been large enough to produce sound to carry throughout a church, but fashion led the way to the tree-trunk pipes of the rumbling bass. Today we see the organ in a more modest role. Other instruments may regain the place they lost. Singing accompanied by strings and woodwind would be a very happy variation, especially in a generation of many school orchestras, and would probably give us a wider range of music than is possible for the guitar. But the willingness to share our musical gifts so that we are not at a performance, not asking how well she plays, but rejoicing together in a variety of music, will help us all to look beyond stereotypes to creativity.

But novelty is not the keynote. Nothing so binds us to the church of history as the hymns we sing which have come down to us from earlier ages of devotion. Of them all there has been no more fertile soil than the Book of Psalms. Subject to many translations, turned into metrical verse, offered in responsive form and the origin of many hymns, these ancient hymns often baffle us while leading our thoughts to the work of God. To me the most difficult element in the Psalms is the direct correlation of obedience/success, disobedience/defeat which runs through so many Psalms, but which does not seem to run through the facts of history or the experience of Christian pilgrims. We know that all too often the most faithful individuals and communities are those who suffer the worst oppression. Of course, there is such wide variety among the Psalms that we also have the most moving account of faithfulness at risk, as in Psalm 73, to set beside the super-confidence of Psalm 91. Indeed, the abiding quality of the Psalms as a source for our devotional singing and praying is precisely the breadth of human experience they enshrine, the mixture of fear, hope, contrition, despair, loneliness, majesty, joy, remembrance and fellowship which is given so powerful a voice, within the context of assurance that God is involved with his world.

To sing our praise is for most of us a key element in worship. Given simple music, literate words and a heart filled with thanksgiving to God most of us can join in congregational singing. For some, the theme will re-echo through the week that follows and provide a focus for private worship also. So let us pick up that hymn book again. It may look a bit weather-beaten and belonging to the solid past. But can't we see there a reflection of our own cry to God?

Lord God, our songs are not like the song of heaven. Our words are often grander than our lives. Our music carries more beauty than our daily actions. Our singing does not come with a singleness of heart. So grant us the power of your Spirit, that our hymns may be honest praise, the song of our lives.

Father, we like old hymns. They tell us of the ageless story of Jesus, and remind us that men and women have been singing your praise since the apostles saw the risen Lord. Thank you for the confidence of faith that comes in old hymns.
Father, we seek to praise you in new hymns. They speak of life in this mixed-up world which challenges all we believe. Thank you for those with vision who write for us of faith to-day.
Father, hear us and bless us as we sing.

Lord, music is a language which we seek to understand. We are for ever grateful for the masters of music who have told of passion and pain and victory and love and the great mystery of your creation. Help us to listen, even when the accent is strange, and find richness in the language of music.

You love the singer, Lord, more than you love the song. When my song of praise is silent, hear what I am.

We all need rhythm, Lord. Waking and sleeping, talking and silence, company and solitude, long vision and close attention. So, as we sing, may the rhythm remind us of the beat of life, breathing your breath, every day, every night.

FOUR

Praying

'My house shall be called a house of prayer,' quoted Jesus in the Jerusalem temple, recalling the words of Isaiah chapter 56. That rebuilt temple, in the prophetic vision, was to be particularly known as a house of prayer for all peoples, not a place for the highly qualified priests, nor for the intense nationalists of Israel, nor for the trading community which then, as now, put up its shop front where the pilgrim crowd was thickest. And a house of prayer is still the name we would love to see given to all our local churches. Places where those with a burden can freely express themselves to the Father of all, where there is a chain of prayer linking us to our parents in faith, where there are no hindrances to the conversation. We are all made so differently that there is never a single recipe which could possibly meet all our needs in prayer. The house of prayer for some will seem a cold shell to others. Those Christian traditions with the most fixed liturgical pattern also acknowledge the place of private devotion, for the fixed forms are general tools, proved to be strong in long use, but not expressing all that is in each heart.

That is how a nonconformist tends to view other traditions. An Orthodox would probably respond, 'We have this great rich feast of prayers, filled with beauty and layers of meaning, and we wonder how you live spiritually without it. Are your prayers not thin and spasmodic?' I do not know any wholly satisfactory way of resolving this tension. If we respond that, of course, we use also from time to time the great historic prayers of the catholic church, that is not at all the same thing as living and breathing those traditions as though they are the life blood of the spirit. We become those who pick odd flowers in a garden, not those with their hands in the soil. There are still some URC congregations where it is considered a novelty to say the Sursum Corda, and in others the minister has to say Amen to his own prayer. So to enter in any deep way into the classical traditions is very hard for us. Those of us who can share sometimes in Orthodox or Roman Catholic worship during ecumenical events become pupils.

But we also have a tradition. Extempore prayer is a tradition and is not at all an easy option. All of us find that it demands much self-discipline if we are to express simply and sensibly, briefly and honestly the needs of the hour. I think that this tradition has become less effective among us in recent years, and this is partly due to the sheer excellence of some of the written material now available. It is also due to memories of extempore prayer done badly with too much repetition or that Cook's tour of world trouble spots that some ministers thought was required. It is a precious opportunity in our worship to raise in prayer the people and events most in our hearts that day, and perhaps we can help members of the congregation to share in this type of prayer, just standing and speaking very briefly during the intercessions. This could be embarrassing, especially if there is a very vocal member always present, but preparation in mutual confidence may help us.

It is that sense of a praying congregation that we all seek to make a reality. Nothing is easier than for the minister to utter the words of the prayer while there is no response for the congregation. Then, in fact, we drop into the worst type of sacerdotalism, leaving everything to the minister. 'What a priest-ridden service that was,' said a visiting Anglican bishop to me as we left a properly traditional nonconformist service in a Pacific island. I staggered under the criticism. But it is sometimes a word we need. I have thought that some occasions of the Roman Catholic mass are now more congregational in form than we have experienced. How can we help every worshipper to pray? The words of the minister are only of limited value for it is very hard to catch up with the speech of another and pray it, so to speak, after him. We all try to do this, but it is hard. So we all need helps in this matter and there are four of great value.

1. It has become the custom in some churches for the whole congregation to be provided with copies of some of the

prayers so that either they can follow and ponder the words or say them in unison. The Prayer Handbook published each year by the Council for World Mission has become such a pew prayer aid in a good many places. In others the appropriate prayer from the WCC handbook is used. These sources are particularly valuable in linking us to the world church family.

2. We also use responsive prayers and litanies. This is a matter of great variety, but where there is no written material in the pew it is probably best if the clauses and responses are brief. The great gain is that everyone can participate actively in prayer and this means more concentration. We are saying, Yes, Lord, that is my prayer.

3. Many churches now recognise also the importance of using some of the great classical prayers with which people become familiar and in which they can share. To turn our backs on such a treasury would be an act of folly, like a ship captain who does not believe in charts.

4. There is the value of silence. More and more we discover that to fill the period of worship with words is unnecessary and may even become a barrier to thought. Periods of silence are for many periods of refreshment. Often we may be guided in the use of the time, offered a text or a leading thought for example. Just as the strongly liturgical traditions have gifts to share, so too do the Quakers, for in the silence each person is equally able to pray from the depths of the heart. (There are more thoughts on silence in chapter 8).

Perhaps to state four helps in that way rather suggests a pot pourri type of worship, a little bit of everything to suit all tastes. We know that an effective order of worship is not created in that way. It demands progression of thought and cohesive style. But over a period, and looking at the whole worship life of a congregation, we can see the possibilities for fully shared prayer. It may be, for example, that at the Communion Service we use certain written prayers and a period of silence in a pattern which we follow for a period and then see whether it has been helpful.

Yet the prayers in the order of worship, following the pattern of Invocation, Adoration, Confession, Thanksgiving, Intercession and Petition as they often do, are still only the visible part of the whole complex life of prayer. Much is always private. Who knows our inmost thoughts except the Lord? So we seek to link public and private worship, letting each inform the other. The public acts of worship take on deeper meaning for us when we come with a personal experience of daily prayer. When this is not the case — and I think that for a growing proportion of us it is not the case — then there tends to be an artificiality about our Sunday prayers, a sort of special suit to be worn to create an impression. So we seek renewal in worship which includes the private as well as the public.

But if there is a difficulty for us in prayer it may well arise not so much from any particular forms but rather from the question, What is it for? In a very secular society it is not at all obvious that we may speak with God as with another person. Childish images of God managing a vast interstellar telephone exchange may mock at us. We may react in hurt to some naïve or selfish prayers which ask God to become Father Christmas.

Prayer, I believe, arises from the conviction that this is God's world and that He is involved with it, a conviction we share with people of other religions. Christian prayer is that approach to God which is by means of his approach to us in Jesus. It is our seeking of God's will in the light of what we know already in the Gospel. If the original conviction has not been born in us, then prayer of all descriptions will be a formality and we will see it mainly as a conversation between people. It is when we are convinced that every day we are living within a world which God created and cares for that we need to express to him our longings, fears, dreams, for we know we are ultimately in his hands. Prayer is an expression of our being as those created by God, redeemed by Christ. It is placing ourselves in his way of forgiveness, continually holding up what we are to the standard of what God calls us to be. It is an expression of love. It cannot be teaching God what he does not know or urging him to be more helpful than he would otherwise be. God is not the unjust judge. Rather it is the daily exercise of placing ourselves within the perfect purpose of God, and so sharing in his saving energy which is always seeking hands, voices, brains, hearts to fulfil the Kingdom.

29

Our Father, you are above us, wonderful. We cannot make you in our imagination. We cannot equal you in holiness. You are in heaven and your name is honoured by us all.

Our Father, we long to live in a world where your will is done, which is the home of your justice and truth, where love rules. We believe such a world is your everlasting purpose.

Our Father, we depend on your care for our lives. We have simple basic needs which can be met if we all respect your creation and do not grab at luxury. May we all have the essentials.

Our Father, we are caught up in a pattern of hurt. As individuals and as nations we hurt each other and we hurt you. Enable us to live in the circle of forgivness so that you may welcome us and renew us.

Our Father, we are afraid. When the crisis comes, who can stand? When the world leads us away from you, shall we follow? When our hearts doubt your reality, shall we despair? Hold us, Lord.

Our Father, yes, truly; Father of all, in whom we are one; Father in authority, whom we long to obey; Father in Love, with whom we are at home. We pray, Our Father.

Pray without ceasing, we are urged. Lord, we can hardly start to pray. Life is hectic. There are great pressures on us. Help us to pray. Enable us to see other people and their burdens and pray for them. Open our eyes to see ourselves in the light of Christ and pray for forgivness. So may our lives be filled with prayer.

FIVE

Reading

The open bible has great significance for all Christians, and especially for those who stand in the Reformed tradition. There it is, actually carried in procession in some of our churches, so that the whole congregation may recognise the source of the Gospel. When the Pope visited Canterbury it was the ancient copy of the Gospels which occupied the seat of honour, the throne of Augustine. We encourage the reading of the bible in every Christian home and ensure that it is read aloud in every service of worship. Yet we are often baffled by the bible. It is such a complex work both in its form and its language and its meaning, it comes to us from so distant a social context, its imagery is not ours and its relation to the whole Christian tradition is not always clear. So for many of us the covers remain unopened and we have guilty feelings when the minister says, 'And you all know the story of Gideon...'.

The centrality of bible reading in worship remains. It is central simply because the bible tells us who God is and what is his nature. So to worship God at all means using the understanding given to us in the bible. Without it we might worship a vague Life Force or a sentimental dream or a magical ogre, but not the God of Jesus Christ. As Pascal said of his vision, 'God of Abraham, Isaac and Jacob, God of Jesus Christ and not the god of the philosophers.' The more comprehensive our public reading is the more accurately we shall be able to reflect the understanding of God that is offered to us in the bible. But here we hit our first major tension.

To take a comprehensive view of the Bible means to take assorted views, very diverse emphases and not one systematic statement about the nature of God. Those of us who have tried to preach and teach are accustomed to presenting our belief in the unity of the bible. It is, so we say, all of a piece. It tells, from Genesis to Revelation, of one God who does not change. Old Testament and New Testament are integrally related, and Marcion (who sought to cast aside large portions of scripture) was indeed heretical. There is, however, a good deal to say on the other side. We all make value judgments about the bible, considering that some portions are of greater weight than others. Even if we say that the Holy Spirit enabled the whole bible to be written we would seek to rule our lives by some parts of it while living in virtual ignorance of other parts. To confess this would be healthy for the church. It would cancel the rather hypocritical stance that is often assumed in public.

But if the reality is indeed of great diversity in the bible how do we evaluate it? How can we, stumbling and often insensitive disciples, pick and choose among the texts? The question is not so much what we read and what we leave unread. It is rather what should we treat as normative for faith and what is subsidiary or supporting revelation. The simplest answer for most of us who are not biblical scholars is to focus on Jesus Christ as revealed in the Gospels, and to concentrate there, as the Gospel writers do, on Christ dying and rising from death. It is surely in that event that we witness most vividly the holy love of God, more clearly than in any words of teaching or in the stories of the early church. At that point all the words become secondary and the Word is the action. When we seek to help another person to know something of what the name God means, we cannot do better than to point to such self-sacrifice, such identification with sorrow, such forgiveness and such victory. This, for me, sets the standard by which scripture is valuable in our discipleship. The application of such judgment is very partial, very subject to error, but I believe it has to be made. The stories of Joshua, for example, which tell us that 'the Lord gave Lachish into the hand of Israel and he took it and smote it with the edge of the sword, and every person in it' suggest that God blesses genocide, and this is simply incredible if to accept suffering is the true nature of God. We mentally review the old stories and interpret 'they *thought* this was the instruction of God'. Looking back, after the cross, we must assert that the God who was plainly shown in Christ was the God sought by

Moses and Joshua, and that he had not changed his character in the interim.

But this kind of judgment, this looking for signs of the cross in the whole bible, is not part of the public reading of scripture; it is part of the interpretive process. When we read in worship the actual text is supreme. It stands to judge us. Let us hear the word of God, we say, recalling the phrases about who has ears to hear, let him hear. That hearing is made more practical by the skill of the reader and we are always grateful to those who can read aloud with clarity, verve, expression and no rushing. We are living in a period of many translations of the bible and this is both opportunity and occasional confusion. The opportunity — unequalled since the Reformation — is to hear an ancient text in the common language and so grasp its meaning more fully. The confusion may arise when a congregation has a mixture of versions or where the familiar meaning is lost in a new version. Freshness and familiarity may both be of value, but they are hard to bring together. The scholars debate the accuracy of the many modern translations. Moffatt seems to have largely disappeared, as has Weymouth. The Revised Standard Version has now many literary aids, J.B. Phillips is still most readable, New English Bible wins good opinions for accuracy, the Good News Bible has flashes of powerful colloquial speech, the Jerusalem Bible is loved by many, the New International Version disappoints me as dull reading. But what shall we do about the King James Version which, until fifty years ago, was commonly regarded as the word actually pronounced by the apostles? Pulpit bibles with those florid title pages and massive board covers still abound. For many of us scripture is memorable precisely in that version, and today when I need to check a reference in a concordance I can find it much more readily in the old words.

It seems to me that if we are reading a passage of bible poetry, or one in which there is a good deal of high-flown rhetoric or oratory, then the King James version may still be the most effective to use in public worship, for the distance from our colloquial speech may be quite appropriate. It is when we read direct narrative, simple and colloquial speech, the personal letters of one to another and theological discussion that we need the most vivid modern versions so that meaning is not hidden behind the antique language. There seems to be very little emotional difficulty now about this. The strict dependence of the British Christian on the King James' Version has been broken, and there is a welcome for good public reading in the modern versions.

When we speak like this of both personal judgments applied to scripture and the wide variety of translations, we realise that the room for misinterpretation is large. Traditionally Protestants have regarded the risk as well worth taking so that the individual responsibility may be ensured. Other Christian traditions have been more authoritative. We still regard the risk as worthwhile, but a greater acknowledgment of it may be proper since Protestant mis-reading of the Bible has caused havoc in many places. In China the Taiping rebellion arose from a local mis-reading of the New Testament which elevated a Chinese to the place of the Son of God to whom all honour was due. In South Africa the Afrikaaner interpretation of the Old Testament has enabled the nation to give religious approval to apartheid and white supremacy. There is indeed no guaranteed infallible route to understanding the bible as it speaks to our condition. It is central to worship and to faith, we long to know it well and some of us spend a lifetime in study of it, but there is still something elusive there. The words, just words, speak in a host of ways to the human heart with surprising power, they are seminal.

One of the most powerful evidences of this is the Presbyterian Church in Burma which was born just a generation ago. Christians in Assam were able to send bibles and hymn books in boxes over the border, to circulate among the Chin Hills villages. The discovery of the New Testament was indeed a revelation. A new world suddenly became available. There is a story of official and Buddhist opposition, the residuary influence of various shrines on the hilltops, healings, excitement, a small group of devoted leaders and then suddenly a growing church, now with 30,000 members. Although such a sudden birth of a church is not unusual the particular point in

Burma was the absence of missionaries and the influence of the written word. 'Let us hear the word of God...' is therefore a powerful and risky moment in our lives. We may be challenged as never before, comforted, accused, confirmed, led, broken, healed.

But for this to happen there is always a process of application. The bible, which does indeed come to us from a strange world, remains a stranger until the words have a point of contact with us. Simply to admire it, as a well-known volume once put it, to be read 'as literature' is not possible, for it demands a response. I can remain entirely objective with regard to the characters in a novel, and need make no judgment about Helen of Troy or Julius Caesar, but to read John's Gospel simply as literature would require a heart of stone, for each step in it demands assent or objection. When the bible has spoken to us in such a personal way it is no longer a strange book speaking from the distant past. Its characters become real people and they, rather than the person at the lectern, are speaking to us. Here is an attempt to let some biblical characters speak in a fresh way.

SIMEON

Every week, in faithfulness and hope,
I sang the praises of God and read the holy words.
The voices of the priests were all familiar
and the older rabbis knew me as a regular.
I was one of the fortunate ones,
living near the temple, only a step from Beautiful Gate,
my feet on the narrow road, my window open to the trumpet.
Yet I was always hesitant, shy, silent,
only speaking in the responses
when the great Amen rose up to heaven.
Always I was waiting for something, some one
beyond sacrifice, incense and psalm.

A family stood beside me offering doves
and suddenly I knew.
I knew the baby, I knew the glory,
I knew the pain, I saw the hope,
and the words poured out of me.
My old eyes have seen salvation
for all in the temple and far beyond;
Here is the light for every nation,
the crown of Israel's age-old search.
Now let me be dismissed, O Lord,
for faith has been fulfilled.

I returned the baby to his mother.
The Levites looked at me with shock.
You'd never expect that of old Simeon, they said.

Luke 2:25-32

PETER

I was startled by noise and lights,
and jumped up from sleep,
still disoriented and bumping into trees.
Together we ran to the place where the lights clustered
and a spear glinted.
There we saw the face, the face of Judas,
a well-known face, sharer in the Way, friend!
Yet with a guard on each side
he led the platoon towards the Master, and embraced him.

Lord, where are the angels? Call on the host!
Why forget your mighty power?
Do you want to go off a prisoner?
Why don't you make an Exodus escape
and scatter the servants of Pharoah?

He could rely on me; me, Man of Action!
I caught the sword out of the bundle and charged.
I might have done some real damage,
But after my first thrust Jesus said,
'Peter, put away your sword,'
and I'd only nicked an ear.
Next time, Jesus, I'll do much better,
I'll defend you to the death.
Me, Man of Action!

But I could not defend myself
when the hint of danger came next evening,
so I ran.
Betrayal and denial. Fine friends you have, O Lord.

John 18:11

CLEOPAS

Walking westward in the evening sun
our eyes were dazzled and our feet were slow.
Joined by a stranger we plodded on
and did not stop to ask his name,
but went on chattering.
We spoke of the day of sorrow,
Passover freedom turned into new tears,
as the Lord died and was carried to Joseph's tomb.
And now the body has been snatched away.
Robbers? Romans? Why take his body?

The stranger started explaining the scriptures,
so, when we reached home, we asked him in.
He clarified wonderfully the word of the prophets,
sharing a hopeful light — 'after three days'.
We were ready for supper. He took the loaf.
He asked the blessing. He broke the bread.
Yes, truly, it was the Lord.
He was the stranger talking with us,
and only when he broke the bread
did we notice his scarred hands. Then he was gone.

Speaking out of scripture, breaking bread at the table,
Jesus, you are the minister, you are Word and Sacrament.
You, the guest in the world's homes, are host for the hungry.
Be with us on the road.

Luke 24

PETER

I'm not a visionary man,
more at home in facts and actions,
but that nightmare was so compelling
that I woke up in a sweat, trembling.
Those writhing creatures coming out of the clouds,
a cornucopia of all that's horrid, slimy, obscene,
and a voice saying, 'Here's your dinner, Peter, eat it.'

That morning the meaning became plain,
when three foreigners came calling for me.
They asked for my help with a Roman army officer
going through great religious disturbance.
I went and found the man was genuine;
he wanted to hear, he was ready for the Lord, I baptised him.

What does this mean?
Do you take all my past,
the precious traditions of our people,
our Jewishness, our temple, our pilgrim history,
and say that these don't matter?
What will the fellowship be like, Lord?
Is it to be filled with barbarians,
people who eat pork and don't know one word of the Law?
O God, I feel the solid framework of life is slipping
for you carry me over the great divide,
and the only landmarks left are hills and crosses.

Acts 10

JOHN

Noise and heat were overpowering,
the noon glare bounced off the rocks
as we struggled in the Patmos quarry.
Hammer and chisel were painful to touch.
The shouts of the prison officers made us cringe
and unaccustomed hands grew blisters.
'Square off that block,' I was ordered,
but when I chipped a crack appeared
and the whole block was ruined.
So I was sent for a week of solitary.

Perhaps it was a blessing.
It was quiet.
The yelling of the guards was distant
and I heard cicadas buzzing in the grass.
I heard new voices.
And as I looked across the sea towards Ephesus
and remembered friends and thought of the Lord,
the quarry became the foundations for a new temple.
A temple in white stone, each stone a life,
each column a congregation.
Seven pillars of grace for seven days in the cell
and the refrain that ran through my head,
If you have ears to hear, then listen.
If you have ears, unblock them,
If you have ears, bless the Lord.

Revelation 1:9

SIX

Expounding

It is good to have been able to hear some of those preachers often labelled 'great'. Weatherhead and Sangster, James Stewart and Leslie Cooke — that dates my youth. Those were preachers who certainly had a following. They were fresh and alive, they had a breadth of vision matched by the facility with words which caught the imagination. There are sometimes discreet sighs in church gatherings today as people comment that we don't have great preachers like that anymore. I'm not sure the comment is true. We don't have such famous preachers, but that is hardly the same thing. Perhaps we do have some preachers who speak a lively word with power and grace, but who are unknown outside a fairly small circle. Preaching itself has become devalued.

The main reason is, I believe, quite plain. As a society we have moved out of the era when listening to a lengthy address is normal. In some of the South Pacific islands the orator is still a popular figure, able to command an audience and not giving short measure. In such places the preacher, too, can be sure of a response. I was often delighted when, after morning service, we all retired to sit around the floor in the pastor's house and one elder would ask 'What was the text?' and there would be someone with a bible to read it out. The elder would then give the sermon again in summary or draw out from the flock the message through question and answer. People had actually listened! But relatively few people in British society now listen in that way. Perhaps university students do at lectures and some politicians listening to expert colleagues and judges hearing the speech for the prosecution. Most people, however, have a quite brief span of attention for the spoken word. More and more we need pictures to help us, and we like the speaking to be broken up into small bites. Some regard this as a sad decline in our civilization, a kind of regression to the nursery. The logic behind that thought is that while speech can convey the whole range of ideas and realities from concrete facts to theoretical notions, pictures or films or drama are more limited.

This may not be wholly true. I would not hesitate at all in praising the power of words, the almost magical accretions of sound which send a precise idea from my mind to yours. Yet pictures do more than convey a concrete image, they may also tell of a mood, a joy, an anger (think of Goya), a nationalism, a way of holiness, the maturity of the human spirit and the glories of creation. Rembrandt may expound the gospel with remarkable fidelity; Picasso may teach us the anti-militarist song; Gaugin conveys, perhaps better than most novelists, the lassitude — almost the death wish — as well as the rich beauty of Polynesia in its days of critical culture contact. So I am not predisposed to denigrate the visual. The puzzle for us in modern church life is how this medium may be effectively used in worship, when we have so many centuries of training to concentrate on words.

Here I meet what seems to me one of the hardest legacies of the Calvinist Reformation. Concentrate on words, indeed! How can we help it when the particular strand of Christian life which formed our fore-fathers was enshrined in volume after volume of words, shelf after shelf of theology, as though words in sufficient number might define Christian faith. Because of that literary bias, the place for visual stories, for the statues and stained glass, the robes and colours, the banners and movements which had been such powerful educating forms in the middle ages was much diminished.

Could we, I wonder, have a circulating corpus of good pictures in reproductions so that churches in a district might have a new one several times a year? Some people might catch a glimpse of faith that way and no-one would be imprisoned with a picture they disliked for very long. The district could then hand over a dozen pictures to a neighbouring district to start the round there.

But if the visual element in human communication has become more important with the modern techniques of television and colour reproduction on paper, the spoken word will remain a key element in worship, since this is how the biblical witness comes to us. So in preaching we all seek to use words with delicacy (for they may easily misrepresent the truth), directness and sincerity. There are many books on the art and craft of preaching; this is not one of them. Here we are concerned with the place of preaching in our worship experience as a whole. For a good many of us in the non-conformist tradition the sermon used to be, and may still be, the focal point of our Sunday worship. For the minister it is where the greatest preparation time has been spent and in which all the ministerial qualities are exposed, both good and bad. For the congregation this is frequently the point at which there is personal reaction to the word of God, where the general becomes individual. But should it be the focus? Should the weight and concentration be placed there? Other traditions would place the emphasis on the prayers or the Communion or the silence. Our preaching emphasis derives from the belief that the proclamation of the word of God, receiving that word in all its varied forms but with personal implication, is the heart of the matter.

There are many different objectives which may be in the preacher's mind and disappointment may stem from the expectation which a congregation has. When we go to worship what should we expect? Some of us expect what we would call a 'Gospel message' by which we tend to mean a repetition of the Pauline message of justification by faith, conversion, new life in Christ and hope for eternity, all spelled out with vigour. This is the sermon with a personal appeal, it is the announcement of the Way which pleads, Come and walk in it. It is the sermon which dares to speak of sin and the necessity of God's forgiveness. It is the classic sermon of Peter at Pentecost. There can be no doubt that such preaching of the cross belongs to the central functions of the church. Yet the context for that sermon is not easily found. To preach it to the faithful church members every Sunday as though they have not yet begun life in Christ is almost an insult. The place for it is rather outside the church, beyond the circle of faith. Certainly from time to time we all need to hear this sermon preached as the reminder of our only standing before God, but for its full effect we seek some wider framework.

A second strand in preaching is, I suspect, rather more emphatic in the nonconformist churches today. It is the teaching sermon which assumes that the hearers have entered into Christian life, but seek more understanding of the bible and its implications. We have some splendid teachers of this sort among us. Many ministers have taught their way through the Beatitudes, the Lord's Prayer, the minor Prophets and so on. The Presbyterian tradition of the minister as the teaching elder confirms this role. The style of much of our theological education confirms it too. One of the risks that we run in this style of preaching is the assumption that the raw material, the biblical text, is as vital and interesting to the congregation as it is to the minister. 'Micah has a message of key importance for us today' may be true, but is not immediately obvious. So the transition between the cultures, between the word written and the word made flesh, needs a lot of thought.

Another way of approach is that which is sometimes called 'prophetic'. This is to concentrate upon a current situation and demonstrate how the Gospel brings both judgment and hope to all involved in it. The starting point is the world as we find it. Using the eyes of faith we try to see through the surface skin of publicity or political routine to speak of the corruption which sin brings into the heart of social life. Again this is risky preaching, but has a great tradition behind it. The risk is the individual hobbyhorse of the preacher, imposed from the pulpit on those who cannot answer back. The risk is worthwhile if the conclusion of the sermon is in truth the word of the Gospel addressing the current issue, and not the minister's solution regarding matters on which he is inexpert.

A fourth objective in preaching is quite different, it is to create a mood or atmosphere in which the congregation catches a glimpse of the wonder of God; it is the sermon which almost touches poetry; which lifts us out of our routine into a distant view of the new Jerusalem. There are not many preachers today who carry this through effectively. We have tended to a conversational style and that hardly allows poetry. But I am grateful to those who have spoken in this way.

Just to mention four types of preaching illustrates how varied preaching is. But in this there is a large question. If the regular worshipper listens to 52 sermons a year — or the extremely faithful even hears 104 — how is it possible for each message to remain in the heart? The problem is particularly acute if the messages are all unconnected. Then the church member cannot keep track without a notebook or aide memoire. Educationally we are speaking in ways that have least impact — at random. There would seem to be good reasons for seeking a much more co-ordinated approach. One way of achieving this is to follow a course of themes as in the Christian education handbook Partners in Learning, or a lectionary. Another — which I think is worth attempting — is for the minister and the church meeting to adopt two major themes each year, one for autumn and one for spring. Then the minister plans the preaching around that theme, taking different approaches to it. For example, if the theme selected is 'Our Father', then sermons will follow on the creativity of God, his authority, his love and care for all, the freedom he gives to his children, the concept of fatherhood and motherhood, and the unity of the family. Then there could be sermons on the human family and God's purpose for it. What did 'My Father's House' mean for Jesus, and so on. The musical side of worship could also have the theme in mind. The objective of this method is that by the end of the three-month period the congregation will be conscious of a genuine learning process in which they have been led step by step each Sunday. This is not to suggest that the occasional sermon on something quite different is out of place, but that a regular method is more likely to have an effect.

Effect is, in fact, very hard to assess. That handshake after service with the 'Thank you for the lovely sermon' does not tell us very much about the real contact between preacher and hearer. There was the man who asked me at the church door, 'Do you play cricket?' 'Not since schooldays.' 'What a pity! I was watching your hands. You would be good in the slips.' Perhaps that day the words were powerless. The only real tests of our preaching are first our faithfulness to the Christ of scripture and second our love and understanding of people. The test of our listening is whether we have, with open minds and receptive hearts, sought to hear the authoritative word of God through the stumbling words of the preacher — and having heard have done something about it.

THE PREACHER PRAYS

Whatever good came out of these books of Kings and Chronicles? How do they speak to my world of mortgages and rebellious young people, of electricity bills and repeated strikes? Lord, help me to see in ancient narratives your word about obedience and rebellion, idolatry and spiritual truth, the place of the tribe in the unity of a nation. Give me the skill and wisdom to translate what is ancient for those who will worship this week.

I love my purple passages, O Lord. I mount up with wings like an eagle or an angel and sometimes I am almost eloquent. Let me see how this may be a temptation, a boost for me which does not help your word. Teach me the simplicity of your language, Lord.

Father, I sometimes become obsessed with trivialities, with nice points of the text or details of church order. Help me when I preach to keep to great matters, justice and mercy, life and death, love and community, your glory and your cross, our calling and our life for ever.

THE HEARER PRAYS

We pray, Lord God, for today's preacher. May the words spoken be all of a piece with the life of the people of God. May we see how words and life belong together. So may we not shuffle off the sermon as a string of nice ideas, but let it nourish and change us.

What a host of sermons I have heard. A few have really helped me. Today, Father, may the sermon be spoken for me, for I need your word. Help me to listen.

In every land men and women preach the gospel of Jesus Christ. We pray that where this is a dangerous thing to do the preachers may have courage, humility and faithfulness. Where it is easy and crowds gather may preachers be unsatisfied with the easy word, but proclaim the hard challenge of the cross. May your Spirit enable all preachers to speak the word of life, through Jesus Christ.

SEVEN

Giving

We may have remained silent in the hymns, minds adrift in the prayers, switched off in the sermon, but when we reach the offertory we have no choice but to be active participants in the action of worship. It is a moment which has great symbolic as well as direct meaning. Everyone in church is saying in an appropriate way that in worship we receive from God and also give to God. There is a rhythm or conversation going on. It is not all 'being talked to'. And it is precisely this which may embarrass us, for it is often much more comfortable to remain as a passive audience member than to be called to become an actor. So we may shuffle our way through the offertory, without much thought, parting with small change and so devaluing the event.

The opposite side to this was the style of offertory which was the custom in many South Pacific churches. Here the special offertory was prepared long in advance, perhaps two or three times a year. The village groups would put together their resources and would appear at church on Sunday in uniform, flowery cotton frocks and hats appearing like beds of zinnias in the pews. When the collection was announced each group in turn would start singing with great gusto. The leader would then start his dance down the aisle with two or three of the fattest mothers to support him, until he arrived at the collection plate on the communion table. There he would hold up his envelope and declare in singing tones the amount being given. And so on, with competitive fervour, until all the groups had given.

The procedure shocked my newly-ordained sense of liturgical propriety. I even started quoting Matthew about not parading one's giving, not letting the left hand know what the right hand is doing, and so on. Yet looking back I wonder whether the Polynesian Christians did not have the essence of the matter. They gave with joy. It was rowdy and competitive, but very generous, and it was a group affair, not private between a man and his wallet. I would not dream of suggesting that our offertory stewards should dance down the aisle, but perhaps we could allow ourselves a glimmer or two of joy in our giving.

For this is one point where we are able to declare the image of God. He is the supreme giver — of life, light, love and truth — and when we give with love we are closer to his nature than when we are passive. The money that we give has to be symbolic of all we seek to give to God, the talents of hands, eye, voice, intellect, the home and family we offer to him, the work which fills our days, the cultural heritage we have entered into, the very language we speak and the children we nurture. But this symbol which we place on the Lord's Table and dedicate in prayer is also the actual fuel which has to be supplied for the life of the church. So, in a remarkable way, the symbol and the critical reality come together; at that point we live our theology. The result is, in the main, depressing and would indicate that we do not believe with any great passion, and this is general in British churches. We have frequent schemes to raise the level of giving, but even when they have some success we are not set free economically because we start from such a low baseline.

This is a matter of some amazement to Christians from other places. Most Americans who worship with us are embarrassed at the small giving of our majority. In Sweden a General Assembly service (with perhaps 800 or 900 people) expects the offertory to be at least £4,000. In India the gifts of villagers frequently represent a day's food. How is it that in this country we generally give so little? There must be many answers. The presence of an established church which traditionally made small financial appeal to the congregation may have been an influence in the past. We have had a tradition of paying a minimum stipend to ministers and so giving the minimum to meet it. There has also been a general rejection of tithing as an Old Testament precept or as an impractical claim. I was shaken in one conversation with Christians from a tithing tradition to be told, 'Why do you talk about 150 members to support one

49

minister? We only need ten families who tithe to support a minister and his family.' But if we reject that method we are then left without guidance about the level of giving to the work of the church, except for the urging of our own church authorities, and this too readily sounds like a distraught mother trying to persuade awkward children to behave.

We know, in fact, that exhortation is very unlikely to produce the dramatic lift in giving which is needed. It is only a dramatic faith-experience which will alter our attitude in a major way, a new vision of God, a new hearing of his claim upon us, a new understanding of solidarity with the world church. I have had the great opportunity to travel widely in the world church and I have noticed that on returning from a poor part of Asia, for example, I have very powerful feelings of guilt about our western luxury expenditure. Yet after two or three weeks of suburban life I get back to normal and do not feel the same pressure to give up my own luxuries. The mood of our context invades the heart and most of us give in. How greatly we need the strength of God's Spirit so that we may live out those convictions which are given to us through participation in the Christian fellowship. But perhaps one standard of judgment does come through at this point. If we could add up the family expenditure on luxuries during the week — the sweets and tobacco and drinks, the entertainment and so on — then it would seem wholly unworthy for our giving to the church to be less.

There is another side to the coin — or preferably to the note. A national church which does not present a clear picture of its finances will not convince people that it needs money. We have not always done very well at this point. We have left people with a hazy impression of the budget, a pudding made up of staff costs and office machinery, as resolutely unattractive as a pantomime dance. In a local church the local budget is obvious to all, for everyone knows that it costs money to heat and light the building, to print the order of worship, to buy new seats for the hall, and to support the ministry. But a denominational budget is bound to be harder to understand. In the URC we have not inspired one another by using the name Unified Appeal, although most people in the church now know that it refers to our support of world mission and our national costs as a church. I think of it as our Sharing Fund, the way in which every member shares in the world church and in wider ministry. We can itemise it like this —

S   Students and training
H   Housekeeping — the cost of Church House
A   Administration — paying for clerical staff
R   Regional Ministry through Moderators
I   International Mission, mainly through CWM
N   National witness — ecumenical sharing
G   General Assembly

But even if our educational tools were more attractive, it is impossible to give some of these items the glamour of pioneer witness in Nepal or healing the blind in India. We just have to accept that part of the life of any church is a routine administration which has to be carried through with economy but also with rather scarce skills.

If raising such funds as these becomes for us a matter of taxation, then the battle has already been lost. For there is no joy in taxation, no lift to the spirit, but only an endless struggle to pay as little as possible. I think this is true throughout the world church and is not a British characteristic. So we seek ways of presenting a challenge, telling the story and allowing the response to come as freely as possible. Sometimes, for example, when the offertory is announced we can describe precisely one of the purposes for which the money will be used. Or we can have a poster in the porch which shows the faces of some of the people we are supporting. For it is always the more personal appeal that makes us want to respond, and when we raise money to pay staff costs of various sorts it should not be difficult to describe a person at the end of the chain whose work we are making possible.

So the offertory is a critical moment in worship. It is necessary for the proper pattern of response. Even if our church should inherit a great legacy tomorrow we shall still take up an offering at each service, for we need to demonstrate that there is a personal response to the gifts of God in Christ. The scale of our giving needs regular and critical revision. The purpose of our giving needs to be described with directness. Then we can indeed come to the offertory with conviction and joy, glad that we can offer some sign of our commitment to the life of the Spirit in the context of our praise.

Jesus Christ, though he was rich, for us became poor so that we through him might receive the riches of the Kingdom. Thank you, Father, for your giving to us. Bless this giving for your purpose in the world.

We are always in trouble about money, how to earn it, how to spend it, how to save it, how to give it. Money troubles us, Lord. Heal our concern and set us free from foolish longings.

This offering of money takes only a moment and does not cause us pain. May we also learn to give ourselves, which takes a lifetime and includes a cross.

Were the whole realm of nature mine, that were an offering far too small. We cannot give enough to express or gratitude for Christ. We give this small sign with thankful hearts.

May this money be used in your service, Lord, for the healing of men and women, for upholding the witness of the church, for extending service to our community and for preaching the gospel everywhere.

Almighty God, we believe that our offering can help your saving purpose. May it be used with imagination and courage, with honesty and hopefulness, and with a loving spirit.

He who sows sparingly will also reap sparingly, and he who sows bountifully will also reap bountifully. (2 Cor. 9.6). May your sowing, Lord, in pain and love reap a great harvest throughout your world.

EIGHT

Eating and drinking

It is a sign of the earthy character of our faith that the central feature of most Christian worship is eating and drinking. Of course, there is a place for food and drink in many religions. The holy meal, offered to idols, consumed by priests, hallowed by prayers, features in diverse cultures from the witches' brew upwards. Food has a mystic quality for some. It is the energy or dynamic which enters into human life. Where food is scarce it is seen as gold is seen in western culture, the primary standard of what is valuable. When we see Buddhist monks begging for their daily food in so many Asian cities, we are reminded that to give food to those who need it is a sign of our common humanity. I remember seeing such a morning parade in Mandalay by the dramatic walls of the ancient palace, with the novices, perhaps twelve years old, carrying their mini-begging bowls as they learnt the humility of the beggar. Food is religious in such a context. So for us the eating and drinking at Communion is both utterly simple and common and physical and a religious experience which is central to faith.

From the beginning it was the most distinctive element in Christian worship. Prayers and hymns, readings and sermon, the offertory and the blessing, all were familiar in form, if not in content, to Jews in every synagogue. The Communion meal, even though it echoed the Passover, was the great novelty in Sunday Christian worship and became the family meal of the church. But what exactly is the family? Is it the local congregation present on that Sunday, or the whole local membership including the absent ones? Or is it something far wider than that, the entire Christian community, all who call God 'Our Father'? The family cannot be less than that, it is the universal church which spans centuries and continents. So even in the small church fellowship we participate in a tremendous action as we receive bread and wine. The liturgy is an expression of just this sense of universality.

There are some daunting consequences. The first is about church unity. If the family of Christ is divided as regards the hymns we sing or about translations of scripture, or about bishops or councils or money, that is a sad reality. But to be divided at Holy Communion is a special sorrow, for that is precisely the point at which all Christians are called to be united with the one Lord. Division there is equivalent to breaking the body of Christ all over again. We know this sorrow whenever we gather in inter-church meetings and find that we cannot share the Eucharist as a crown of our fellowship. Christians who have never felt this sorrow have not yet entered into the ecumenical movement with passion.

A second consequence is that the family brings with it obligations. We have to be aware of the needs of the whole family and not only of our own hunger. The risk of making a private and selfish communion meal was there from the start. So Paul accused the Corinthians. 'It follows then that when you are assembled in one place you do not eat the *Lord's* supper. For everyone tries to grab his food before anyone else, with the result that one goes hungry and another has too much to drink! Haven't you houses of your own to have your meals in, or are you making a convenience of the church of God and causing acute embarrassment to those who have no other home' (1 Cor. 11:20-22). There was an absence of any real expression of the Christian fellowship. But, even with all our dignity, it may be so today. To live in one corner of the church as though another part does not exist is just as dangerous for spiritual health as the rowdy table at Corinth. We can only come to the table if we are aware of sisters and brothers in hunger, pain and oppression and if we offer to them whatever they need of our resources.

There is a third aspect of the family at the table, and that is the empty chairs. The family is not complete. Always we are conscious that the church or Christian fellowship is only a small part of the human family which God calls to participate in his feast of life. If we celebrate in a holy corner, or in any spirit of smugness, then we narrow down the inclusive love of God and turn the cross into a private totem. The gift of God in Christ is for all, so the sign of that giving is also for all who can receive it. The nature of the family is thus a declaration of the Gospel.

When we think of the development of the Eucharist from the early days of the church, there is still a good deal that we regret. Within the Roman tradition the service gathered aspects of the secret mystery religions, with the priest as the one who knew how to handle the sacred food. Thus the koinonia or fellowship nature of the feast, which seems to have been distinctive in the early years of the church, slipped into the hierarchical and formal style which became standard for most of Christian history. We are still grateful for the Reformation insight which gave the feast back to the people and delivered it from much superstition. This insight has also informed the Roman Catholic church in recent years so that in many places the mass is truly a people's service. The place of the minister or priest is not to act as guardian of the sacred mysteries as though he has a formula which is a private jargon. Rather it is to welcome the people in the name of Christ, to share the words of forgiveness, to pray for the Holy Spirit and to represent the breadth of the fellowship. It is the authorisation of the church given to the minister in his ordination that he should speak in the name of Christ at this point in our worship, so that Word and Sacrament are bound together in the commissioning.

So we seek to emphasise the fellowship quality of the sacrament, demonstrating that we are a company of Christ's people. The fellowship is to the context for the presence of Christ. I find it hard to follow the sacramental theology of the Catholic tradition which speaks so much of 'real presence'. Can there ever be an unreal presence of Jesus Christ with his people? Are we not confident that his promise stands and that he is with us? 'Real' cannot be taken as the opposite of 'unreal'. It can only make sense if it means 'sure, clear, made known to us.' Eating and drinking is a real experience, something actually happens to us, and in it Christ comes to each of us in all the agony of death and all the strength of victory. Our remembering is actual present growing in our pilgrimage, and Christ steps out of history to be with us on the road. This is the testimony of the church through the ages, and we rejoice to find it true for us.

Yet we have strange inhibitions and hesitations. There are three practical matters which cause great discussion and sometimes dismay. The first is the frequency of communion. We now have in the URC three traditions. The former Presbyterians often held to quarterly communions, the former Congregationalists to monthly, and the former Churches of Christ to weekly. I find the concept of very occasional communion hard to understand. It is generally claimed to be a way of emphasising the importance of the occasion, to make it very special. But does rarity have that effect? Would it not be equally logical to say that the sermon is so important that we should only hear one a year? I think the weekly Communion does come closest to the New Testament pattern, and the freedom we enjoy in the URC makes it possible for us all to experience it.

A second matter which is much discussed today is the place of children at Communion. Most churches are moving tentatively to an invitation to the children of members to share if they wish to do so. On one side of the discussion are those who see baptised children as members of the church, as an essential part of the fellowship, and therefore welcomed by Christ to his table so that they may grow in knowledge of him. On the other side are those who would wait for a personal declaration of faith and a measure of maturity in understanding, lest the communion be treated lightly or foolishly. Since we are all beginners in understanding the nature of Christ's presence with us, it is very difficult to see the absence of intellectual understanding as any bar. Perhaps it is the whole nature of the fellowship which is challenged. If the relationship of children and adults is open, then it will be natural for all to sit together without any straining for effect.

A very practical matter which has caused quite a lot of difficulty is the nature of the elements themselves. Grape juice or wine, wafers or bread? Is it significant? Can we pick and choose those elements which are most convenient? The question of alcoholic or non-alcoholic wine has caused some quite major problems in ecumenical progress. The church in militant Moslem states has met a ban on alcohol. In some parts of the Pacific islands there is still such a folk memory of the total dissipation of the population when alcohol was first introduced on whaling ships that a teetotal church is regarded as essential. Coconut juice was commonly used for wine and always seemed to me a very natural replacement. But those who read the New Testament in a very literal way will insist that 'Do this' must mean drinking wine from grapes, although they often accept a wafer as substitute for bread. I do not believe that too severe a literalism is required of us by the Gospel. Clearly, if we can receive actual wine and actual bread, then this is the nearest we can get to the primitive life of the church, but if for any reason that is not possible, then I do not believe the Holy Spirit will be absent because we use a substitute.

As with the offertory the Communion causes us all to be active participants. The theology of Christ, crucified and risen, is brought to a sharp focus when we actually do something together. The doing is the key, the theology is our meditation about it. But the doing is a very easy, common thing, just eating and drinking. So this part of our worship is joined to the universal experience of food and drink, hunger and thirst. What we do in church is not wholly separated from the daily life of the world or from the agonies of those thousands who have no bread today. There is a distinction between Communion bread and the food needed for filling all the empty bellies in the world, for Jesus distinguished bread for the day and the living bread which is God's gift for the life of the human spirit. But the two must not become separated. To eat the bread at the Lord's table must be a sign that we recognise hunger as an enemy of the Kingdom. Krister Stendhal, an American scholar, said of the sheep and goats parable in Matthew 25 that Jesus told this story 'to indicate that the beleaguered and persecuted are so precious in God's eyes that the whole world will be judged by how they, the oppressed, have been treated. So precious, so decisive, so religious, so theological is food for the hungry.' Communion bread is holy, but so is that bread which rescues from starvation.

It is connections of that sort which remind us of the Communion as the word demonstrated. There is an old phrase about the 'evangelical ordinance'. Sermon and Supper both speak of God's love in Christ, the one through the mind and voice of the preacher — and thus liable to error — and the other through an action which all share — and which is liable to misinterpretation. We are not offered infallibilities, but open doors through which we may enter the life of Christ. But Communion continues to speak, and the Melbourne WCC Conference in 1980 expressed it like this:

Where a people is being harshly oppressed, the Eucharist speaks of the exodus or deliverance from bondage.

Where Christians are rejected or imprisoned for their faith, the bread and wine become the life of the Lord who was rejected by men but has become 'the chief stone of the corner'.

Where the Church sees a diminishing membership and its budgets are depressing the Eucharist declares that there are no limits to God's giving and no end to hope in him.

Where discrimination by race, sex or class is a danger for the community, the Eucharist enables people of all sorts to partake of the one food and to be made one people.

Where people are affluent and at ease with life, the Eucharist says, 'As Christ shares his life, share what you have with the hungry.'

Where a congregation is isolated by politics or war or geography, the Eucharist unites us with all God's people in all places and all ages.

Where a sister or brother is near death, the Eucharist becomes a doorway into the kingdom of our loving Father.

In such ways God feeds his people as they celebrate the mystery of the Eucharist so that they may confess in word and deed that Jesus Christ is Lord, to the glory of God the Father.

59

BEFORE COMMUNION

Father, we cannot come as righteous guests to your table. We do not deserve a place with the friends of Jesus Christ. But we believe you call us to come, seeking to feed us with the bread of life, renewing our faith and joining us to the whole fellowship of your people. Today and always we are thankful for your invitation.

We do not understand all that Communion means. There is a simple service with many depths of meaning. Help us today to hold on to the meaning that will speak personally to our need, the very word of the Lord and his presence to renew and strengthen us. May this be your blessing because you are here, Lord.

I'm not sure that I should come to the Table. I know it is a holy meal and I am not at all a holy person. Perhaps I had better stay away. But is it your way of saying welcome, even to me? Are you really rubbing out those awful things in my record? Do you prefer to sit with sinners? Will you feed me as a friend? Lord, this is wonderful and I thank you.

DURING COMMUNION

Bread which has been broken....
Your body broken by violence, by cruelty, by prejudice and bigotry. Your body broken by the vested interests of those in power. Your body broken by friends who deserted and betrayed you.
Your love amazes me.

Your body broken by the indifference of people in all ages, by such resolute refusal to understand your word, by arrogance in church and state and by our wars within the human family.
Your love continues still.

Your body broken and shared to those who believe in every place; your people called to be your body today; your body on the cross in the midst of this life. Your love includes us all.

Wine which has been poured....
Your life offered up as a gift; your agony at the end; your final trust in the Father; your obedience at every step, pointing us to the true life for humanity.
Your life is for us.

Your life bringing light to the darkness within us; your life for our systems of death; your life which takes our burden and suffers all things that we may have life indeed.
Your life is new creation.

Your blood, sign of life, shed at Calvary, that day is far away and yet is here. So you are here. Your blood, not the sign of death and defeat but of loving victory. We need your life in us, O Lord.

AFTER COMMUNION

It is good to be here. Let us put up a tabernacle and stay here. But that is not your way, Lord. You lead us out of the service of worship to carry your word and your spirit into our homes and the places where we work. Enable us to do this faithfully whatever happens during this week.

Gracious Father, you bind us together with a common meal. You make us one with your whole church everywhere in all ages. We pray that we may never break your body by selfishness or distrust, but may show the spirit of fellowship in our lives.

I came to your table, dear Lord, with a burden. May I leave with the absolute certainty that you are with me, carrying the burden too.

NINE

Silence

We are no longer surprised that the Quakers value silence in worship so highly for most of us have discovered that it is a very valuable part of our praise. Silence is a valuable commodity in hectic lives. It is bliss for noise-battered lives. In worship it is relief from the spate of words. Always it is leading towards a different sort of listening, the inward ear that hears the silent pain or longing or hope prompted by the Spirit. Most of us find that the discipline of silence is very demanding, so we do not attempt more than a minute or two in a service of worship. Longer periods might be more creative, but we certainly need help in using them. What do you do with wandering thoughts?

There is usually a clear starting point for our periods of silence. It may be the bible reading or one verse of it, or a hymn we have just sung, or a special theme for the day, or particular people whom we have in our minds, or it may be a great problem hanging over us or over the church, or a picture we hold in our hands. The leader of worship may indicate the starting point, or punctuate the silence with a brief word to remind us of it. This is non-directive. It is just providing signposts for us to help us find a path, acknowledging that the use of silence is very individual so that each one is making a different journey, holding up different thoughts to the same light of the Gospel. But those starting points are important. They may determine whether our silence is introspection, self-examination, or looking towards others. They may give us fresh thoughts that we badly need and carry us out beyond the domesticities of life.

The wandering thoughts, however, may meander with such aimlessness that the silence carries us nowhere in particular. It is helpful to some of us to have a method of using the time. Many have been suggested by those of other traditions and here I can only sketch a few.

The Daisy Pattern

We have a starting point and let our thoughts develop freely from what it suggests to us, but then consciously return to the starting point again. In this way we can develop several different meanings of a text or theme, but make full use of what is given. We do not feel guilty about wandering thoughts; instead we use them.

The five finger exercise This is where we actually use our fingers as a reminder of the progression of thought. There are various lines this can take.

The theme applied to myself

to my family and friends

to the church

to the whole community where I live

to the international fellowship

Here we have expanding circles of thought. If the starting point is a verse from the Gospels, then the five fingers may be counted like this:

What was Jesus saying and doing?

How did that affect the people around him?

Is Jesus saying or doing the same for us today?

How can I respond?

How can I share this Jesus with others?

The spiral This is a way of starting, not at any given point, but with the varied and often haphazard thoughts we have of the recent past. We just think about our lives, our friends, the news that has struck us, the events we have enjoyed or suffered until we recognize one item about which we should pray, and then we concentrate on that, seeking to understand the grace of God touching that person or situation.

We can all find patterns of silent prayer which suit our needs and these methods are simply suggested as possible guides. We realise that silent prayer is typical of private prayer. So in public worship the use of silence helps to link Sunday with every day and can help to train us in the use of private times of prayer or meditation. One risk of the longer periods of silence is introspection, when we become totally absorbed by ourselves, so it is good to set silence in the context of public worship when there are ample reminders of the needs of others.

These are very practical matters. But there are two aspects of silence which lead us deeper into the nature of worship.

The first is our dread of silence. Many of us fear it and make sure we do not often find it. So background noise or music is often provided, more and more people walk our streets with music pouring through their headphones, and we tend to think of silence in terms of isolation and death. As silent as the grave. As silent as an ice age when not even a leaf can stir and shake. As silent as the immensity of interstellar space. Silence means a nothingness, for the processes of life break the silence. But we can move beyond such dread if we recall the presence of God in silence. God's presence does not depend on sound waves. There are many testimonies to the impact of the Holy Spirit during periods, long or short, of silent prayer. 'It just came to me,' or, 'I suddenly realised...' or 'My eyes were opened'. While we know that human voices and written words are normal vehicles for the mystery of the will of God to reach us, the silence is also open to Him and is not the death of his voice. Indeed it may well be that the quietness sometimes helps us to hear even better than the noise of praise. 'After the wind there was an earthquake, but the Lord was not in the earthquake. After the earthquake came a fire, but the Lord was not in the fire. And after the fire came a gentle whisper.' (1 Kings 19:12 NIV). So it may well be that the noise of worship stirs some to the depths of their hearts — whether a Bach cantata or a Caribbean chorus — but that for others the fullest communion with Him who is nearer to us than breathing, requires silence.

But, paradoxically, we never know complete silence or stillness. In all our waking hours we live with movement. It is not just that the heart is pumping away. Rather it is the constant shouting within us which can actually give us a headache.

For, when we are even dimly aware of the immensities of life, the immediacies fight for a place. The pains and sorrows of short lives, the strivings of sex, the enormous imagination with all its dread of the future, hunger, the excitement of expanding knowledge, the lingering antipathy for those who hve hurt us, the regret about hours wasted — all these and many more become, as it were, the voices which speak endlessly in our hearts. At times they shout. Our peace may be destroyed not by the pressure of voices from outside but by these inner voices which claim our attention and obedience. So we need awareness of these familiar notes in the interior orchestra if we are to hear through them the calling of the creator, and not confuse the passions of everyday with the passion of Christ. God is not contained in my spirituality any more than in my physical senses. He is seeking me through both.

Throughout Christian history there have been contemplative orders and individuals who have developed the use of silence; no doubt we have much to learn from them. But perhaps in the Reformed tradition we need to find our own ways of using this gift of silence in close association with our understanding of the word of God. Before the expression comes the thought. The word comes to us in Christ, the word is preached and the sacraments act the word, but the silence may be the word germinating, putting down roots and beginning to occupy the space of our minds, so that in time we may become a word to others.

All this leads us back to the biblical witness where quietness and stillness are contrasted (as in Isiah 30:15) with the busyness of those who strive to fight every human battle with human resources. 'Be still' sang the Psalmist, because the ultimate order of the universe, beyond all the raging of the nations, is the presence of the creating, sustainaing Lord. 'Be silent, all humanity, before the Lord' said Zechariah, and in that mood of wonder even the chorus of angels and saints and elders before the throne was silent for half an hour. (Revelation 8:1). So our silence may be praise, a true part of worship, a relief from speakers, a time to know ourselves, an opportunity to hear that inward testimony of the Spirit.

TEN

Blessing

And now may the grace of our Lord Jesus Christ.... Relax, it's over. We have completed the ritual and can go out to get a breath of air. Those last words of the service are sometimes a formula that spills from the lips and trickles into the ears without meaning. Why do we use them? The root of this part of the liturgy goes back to Genesis and all the blessings given to and by the patriarchs. Israel was to be a blessing, Moses gave a blessing to the tribes and so on. A glance at the concordance shows how often the characters of ancient Israel blessed others, and how 'to be blessed' was the longing of all pilgrims. In the Psalms, in worship, we find 'bless' 43 times and 'blessed' 40 times. It was, therefore, a very natural carry-over into the apostolic church for the elders or leaders to give a blessing, that is to call for the gifts of God to be with those blessed. It has often been pointed out that the Christian blessing is more than a prayer. It is not saying, 'Please God, give these people grace, mercy and peace'. It is rather a declaration, an announcement that God's grace, mercy and peace are now given to you. The Blessing is a triumph of faith. When we say and hear it with all its meaning it is the moment when we confess the reality of spiritual gifts, just as though the offertory is being reversed.

The blessing most commonly used today is that with which Paul concludes 2 Corinthians. It is trinitarian in form and simple in words, so is very easily remembered and spoken together. Many other blessings occur in the New Testament. For example:

Grace to you and peace from God our Father and the Lord
    Jesus Christ. (Romans 1:7, 1 Corinthians 1:3)
The God of peace be with you all. (Romans 15:33)
The Grace of the Lord Jesus be with you. (1 Corinthians
    16:23)

Grace to you and peace from God the Father and our Lord
>Jesus Christ who gave himself for our sins to deliver us
>from the present evil age, according to the will of God
>our Father, to whom be the glory for ever and ever.
>(Galatians 1:3-5)

The grace of the Lord Jesus Christ be with your spirit,
>brethren. (Galatians 6:18)

Peace be to the brethren, and love with faith, from God the
>Father and the Lord Jesus Christ. (Ephesians 6:23)

Grace, mercy and peace from God the Father and Christ
>Jesus our Lord. (1 Timothy 1:2)

May grace and peace be multiplied to you in the knowledge
>of God and of Jesus our Lord. (2 Peter 1:2)

These give the clear indication of how the apostles baptized a
Jewish custom into the Christian community. God the Father
and God the Son are constantly mentioned together as the
giver. Grace, peace, mercy, love, fellowship are gifts being
shared. Where an ancient blessing might have been for pro-
sperity or many children, the apostolic blessing witnesses to a
shift in theology. God, as we know him in Jesus, is eager to give
his children these gifts of community, serenity, courtesy and
self-sacrifice.

The grace of our Lord Jesus Christ. The word is elusive, but
brimming with suggestions. In English we connect it with the
concept of graciousness (Her Royal Highness, with that
graciousness so characteristic of her, comforted the little boy...)
and the use of the word in a ritual form of address (Your Grace,
we humbly submit...), both suggesting qualities from on high.
We have also transposed the word to take the place of 'blessing' when we say 'Let us say grace'. These uses do not directly
uncover for us the original Greek word, but they are helpful ad-
ditions, adding to the richness of the word. I think that we
would have to use quite a long phrase to give an adequate
English meaning, something like 'The gift of God in Christ by
which he creates in us the ability to become like him.' It is a
transforming or reforming gift. It is the gift of the living water
and the living bread in John's Gospel, the new nourishment of

the human spirit, by which the quality of God's eternal life is born in us. 'Out of his full store we have all received grace upon grace; for while the law was given through Moses, grace and truth came through Jesus Christ.' (John 1: 16-17 NEB). This verse emphasises the nature of grace as God's gift which is in Jesus Christ. The law stressed the divine demand, Jesus brings the new power to respond, the authority to forgive and the spirit to incorporate us in his risen life. Many people have been a little suspicious of the John Henry Newman verse:

> And that a higher gift than grace
>   Should flesh and blood refine,
> God's presence and his very self
>   And essence all-divine.

This suggests a poor view of grace, as though it is a Christmas parcel, done up in the neat wrapping paper or bible or sacrament, and to be clearly distinguished from the presence of God in Christ. I do not believe the two can be separated. It is the presence and the very self which is grace. That is the new promise and the blessing of God on all who turn in faith to him.

As we begin to experience the love of God, we are led into wonder, love and praise at the dimensions of the love of God — breadth, length, depth and height — which surrounds our life. Breadth tells us of the universal care of God for the whole of creation, without respect of race or religion. This reality was foreshadowed in Old Testament faith, though hidden at various points in the history, but it becomes evident in the experience of the apostolic church. The love which watches over sparrows, prodigals and tax collectors is broad enough to include Romans and barbarians, slave and freeman, elderly Britons and puzzled school children. No person and no part of creation is outside that love. Length speaks of patience, going to any length in order to rescue the crazy wandering sheep. It is love which does not alter with the centuries, but is as vivid and personal as when Jesus touched a leper. When we have a glimpse of our own stubbornness, then we rejoice that God has not given us up long ago, but perseveres with us despite disappointment. Depth is a word which gathered new meanings in the work of Paul

Tillich. The depth of our being is the point at which we know God, in the ultimate challenge, the absolute standard, the deepest distress and hopelessness. Even in the depth of the sea (as far from blessedness as a Jew could imagine) the love of God is present. We cannot fall below the hands of God. Nor can we rise above him. In the height of joy, success, victory, bliss, mutual love, great insight when we sense the crown of life we still meet the love of God, rejoicing with us. It is love of those dimensions that is to be with us, our great ground of confidence.

The fellowship of the Holy Spirit. There is no solitary salvation in the bible. Always the individual is part of a family or a tribe or a community and salvation has that communal aspect. So we do not receive a blessing as though it is a personal cheque for our private account. We are blessed by God in a fellowship, a network of relationships, in which we are well known, where our joys and sorrows are understood, where we can partake in caring for others. Such fellowship was experienced by the apostles and early church as a gift of the Spirit. It did not arise out of their wisdom or good preaching, nor was it created by any rule book, and it seemed to them a gift which they could only receive with thanksgiving. It was not easy to receive. When it meant Jew and Gentile sitting down to a meal at the same table the human spirit revolted, as Paul reminds us in Galatians. In exactly the same way there are places where the human reaction now is to object to black and white eating together although that fellowship is a gift which the Spirit seeks to give. Indeed, the fellowship of the Spirit is precisely that community which is not created by our natural tribalism, it is rather a trans-cultural fellowship which, in a surprising way, holds together those whom instinct or habit or law would tend to keep apart.

The blessing is thus an affirmation that the great gifts of the gospel are with us. We do not have to live always in the 'jam tomorrow but never jam today' type of religion, as though a tough, barren, sorrowful life will one day be over, to reveal bliss hereafter. The blessing is for today. We are assured that the most wonderful spiritual treasures — which generations and civilizations longed for — are with us and in us and between us. Another way in which we sometimes show this is giving each other the Peace, although a certain stiffness in some of our congregations still makes this rather difficult to introduce. But when we can do it naturally we actually offer the Peace to neighbours, assuring them that right now the peace which is beyond human planning is theirs. We can only speak such a blessing if we believe it. It is a test of faith. The last word spoken in our normal Sunday worship is laying hold of the riches of faith by which we can live out a Christian discipleship.

Receive now, O unbeliever, the blessing of repentance as the light shines from the Gospel of Christ.

The Lord's blessing is on this marriage. As his love is reflected in the love which these two have declared, so may his peace defend their hearts and their home, in Jesus Christ.

God's blessing is on these fields, these crops, these workmen as together they fulfil his good purposes in creation. May the blessings of harvest also rejoice our hearts and feed the hungry.

In a cruel day of a sad year, the Lord bless you. His grace, which we know in his suffering, be your support this day.

May the blessing of God be with you in this assembly. The universal care of the Father, the healing strength of Jesus Christ, and the unity of the Holy Spirit be known in all your deliberations.

The Lord bless us in planning this new church. The Lord bless us as we dream of its service. The Lord bless us as we share our resources. The Lord bless us as we wait for its completion.

Blessed are the peacemakers. May the blessing of God be with all who work for reconciliation, who bear the bitterness of both sides, who refuse to accept impossibilities, who see a hope for your kingdom to come. They shall be called children of God.

May the blessing of God be with us in this concert of music, his beauty reach us through human talents. We praise and bless the Lord for the song of the Kingdom which echoes in our ears.

ELEVEN

Routine or Revelation

If you have followed thus far with patience, you will see that we have looked at the main ingredients of our normal Sunday worship. Now, if you have had a cup of tea and feel ready for another exercise, we will approach some of the major question marks that surround our worship today. There could be an endless parade of questions which the angels alone could answer. I am taking a mere handful and only suggesting how we might approach them.

In my mind, and perhaps in yours, there is often a mixture of duty and delight, a routine to be carried and a spirit which carries me. Worship, we we may say in our rebellious moods, is a routine, it is a regular and often boring event which is necessary simply because it holds the church together. It is a duty because we are church members, and because the bible tells us to worship. Real worship, we might be tempted to add, is not such a regular observance, it springs out of the sights and sounds and relationships of life, it is stirred in us by the golden light of evening across the meadows and the whisper of the slow movement of the Emperor Concerto and the shout of a small child leaping into our arms. Then we open ourselves to the indwelling of the Spirit, then we say a silent prayer of true thanksgiving and partake of the life of Christ.

It is a very attractive position to hold, fitting, as it does, the contemporary mood of laissez faire. I suspect that, as with most of our rebellions, there is a small element of truth here, but also a considerable amount of self-deception and muddle. The truth that I recognise is that there are indeed experiences in life which generate a mood of spiritual alertness. This has been recognised in times of great danger, fear, natural catastrophe and approaching death as well as in those moments of beauty and love which, as we say, lift up our hearts to God. We are, in all these experiences, shaken out of our routine security of custom and presented with a new emotional challenge. We cannot respond by paying a bill or catching the train to work, we have to offer some other response of will and energy, of attitude and courage, of spirit. This is a reality for which we thank God. It is part of the fulness of our humanity and not an option which is open to computers. We do get stirred to the depths of our being — though perhaps not as often in modern British society as would be healthy for us.

But to suggest that this could be or should be the main way in which we worship is surely a delusion. I see four reasons for saying this.

1. The key experiences which awaken our spirit do not happen very often and for some people may not happen at all. There is a large measure of routine about most of our lives. Some of us are so protected from world events that war, injustice, violence, hunger never strike us. Some also have very little sensitivity to beauty, perhaps because the daily grind has absorbed so much energy or because the culture has not valued visual beauty highly. (There are some cultures in the Pacific Islands, for example, where the only consideration of beauty is usefulness; the beautiful woman, the one admired, is the one who can weave or sew or plant supremely well. I once stood admiring the sunset and I am sure the local people were discussing my sanity!). So to rely on the heart-stopping moment means a totally haphazard spiritual life, and possibly a non-existent one. Whole passages, whole years slip by and we are never drawn to give thanks to God.

2. To rely on such experience as a guide to worship is too subjective and not clearly focussed on Jesus Christ. If we are expressing, perhaps in silent prayer, our response to a great personal event, then our whole attitude and interpretation may be very distant from the Gospel. The unredeemed part of me may take over. Prayer then very readily becomes a selfish plea that, regardless of what happens to others, I may be kept safe. Self-generated worship is likely to reflect the self, and that is not always very Christ-like. G.K. Chesterton has a passage in his lively account of Francis of Assisi where he writes about natural religion:

The immediate effect of saluting the sun and the sunny sanity of nature was a perversion spreading like a pestilence. The greatest and even the purest philosophers could not apparently avoid this low sort of lunacy. Why? It would seem simple enough for the people whose poets had conceived Helen of Troy, whose sculptors had carved the Venus of Milo, to remain healthy on the point. The truth is that people who worship health cannot remain healthy.

(G.K. Chesterton, *St Francis of Assisi*,
First published 1923, Hodder and Stoughton, 1944)

3. The spasmodic worship of the individual provides no public witness. However few we may be at church on Sunday it is a public event and therefore an evangelical event. Without it the whole community would lose one of the marks — even if a rather undynamic one — of the spiritual dimension of life. Restrictions on public worship are common in countries where the government seeks to support another religion or to empty life of religion. To allow public worship to wither and die simply from inattention or from irrelevance would be to do the work of those who, for all sorts of reasons, advertise its demise. If we are to find that base of fellowship from which a new social evangelism may spring, then corporate worship surely has a part to play.

The word fellowship points very clearly to the other failure of private vision as the staple of worship. On our own we see only a small segment of the rounded reality of Christ, the Word of God, the Lamb of God, the Way, the Truth, the Life. We see only what is born in us by our own experience. But the personal view always needs correcting by the fellowship so that bias and ignorance can be balanced by others. We need that comprehensive experience of how God speaks to us in Christ. We desperately need a network of relationships in which we may express all we mean by love and forgiveness. And we also need the background of Christian history which warns of so many false dawns and introduces us to the work of so many saints of God. Corporate worship is thus an essential aspect of faith. To be alone with the birds is not a substitute for sharing the bread and wine at the Lord's Table.

Yet despite these solid reasons there remains a valid question about the place of personal, irregular, spontaneous worship. How is it connected with the regular diet? Are not the two frequently at odds with each other? I think, for example, of those who suffer from a rather grim style of Sunday worship with a narrowly biblical language of faith, and who yet, in the realm of music or art or love or travel find an expanding, tremendous vision of the divine nature. The spirit of Schubert on Saturday and the voice of Ezra on Sunday. The message is plain. The regular pattern of worship must be broad and flexible and generous enough to complement the highest achievements of the human spirit, and never descend to the petty or the pedantic. All our prayer books and orders of worship have to be judged by high standards so that they can keep company with the great emotional experiences which raise our sights to the wonder of God's creation. But there is also a challenge to every worshipper. We have to be ready to bring our treasures into worship and not lay them at the door like shoes at the mosque. When there is a family tragedy, for example, we are not asked to forget it on Sunday morning, but to hear the gospel in the light of that experience, to see how each illuminates the other, and to draw on the resources of the songs and prayers of faith.

All this makes us realise again what a demanding business true worship is. I am very thankful for ministers who may be taking the umpteenth service in a row, but who yet come to it with freshness, with the weight of their own new insights and with evidence that pastoral challenges have touched their heart. The Protestant style of worship places a heavy burden on the minister and in the past we have often rejected the published liturgy, believing that what is spontaneous is better. Many of us have learnt that this is not always so. The burden can be too heavy and then the standards may slip alarmingly. So most of us are grateful for elements of published orders of worship which bring to us a universal word. Routine can mean boredom. It can also mean strength. Those of us, whether in pew or pulpit, who are regular enough attenders to know the routine pray to the Holy Spirit that the latter may be true for us.

Here are some meditations on experience through our physical senses which may lead us, not to forget God, but to praise him for the gift of such a wonderful world.

Touch

Textures may alert us to the substance. There is a smoothness of rounded pebbles wet with the sea which yet have a hint of grittiness when they dry. The cat's fur could not be smoother when stroked from the head backwards, but to push against the grain means spiky objection. All fur is such a complex thing to touch, responsive to our fingers, a million springs to clasp our hand. There is a very distinctive touch to old furniture; that ancient oak table, polished through centuries of use and care, has a depth to its polish and all the little irregularities of grain which no formica ever imitates. There are splendid contrasts. The shell of the horse chestnut, spiky and irregular, and the nut just newly bursting out, with its high gloss, a precision tool. There are all the touches of skin, in greeting, in love, in home and hospital care which tell us of the bones beneath and the years of wear and the work that hands have done.

Touch introduces us to use. The typewriter keyboard which has become very familiar so that no replacement is ever quite the same. The steering wheel. The saw handle which exactly fits my grip. Those special knives and forks, kept for days with visitors, which have an unexpected edge in the hand. The violin and its bow, each with its own quality and fit; the left hand finding the very different touch of each string, the right extended by the bow's grace and firmness. The blind touching the braille page.

Touch and memory. Whatever happened to starch? That first tropical suit of white cotton drill, starched and ironed for Sunday, almost standing up on its own like a suit of armour, with a gloss on first wearing.

Touch and shock. Unexpected irregularity in a flight of steps, and my whole leg jars because the surface is just an inch from the expected. Picking up a shell in the evening and finding in it a hermit crab. Feeling and not looking in a drawer, touching that sharp knife blade, feeling the blood before any pain.

Reach out your hand and touch my hands and my side. For every touch of the Lord, lift up your hearts.

Sound

What an infinite richness! The sound of music in all its forms. The symphony orchestra tuning up, audience chattering on crescendo, then drifting into silence as the leader takes his seat and gives the final A; a pause, the conductor comes on, applause, bow, attention, and in the silence the woodwind announce a theme. The music that has stirred us, our personal desert island discs. Kathleen Ferrier singing 'He was despised' from Messiah. That extraordinary Polynesian chanting when the men carry the strong theme and the women go off into odd descants as the mood takes them, shaking with energy and delight. My first real hearing of Beethoven on the old 78s in an Air Force camp in Egypt; Bruno Walter and the Vienna Philharmonic; passion and order. My wife singing 'Linden Lea' at a church concert. Then a whole world of pop and rock which is just noise to me, but is a realm of pleasure to my son.

The Swiss hillside and cowbells, marrying sound and sight in the harmony of altitude. The air raid siren, the ambulance siren, the police car wail. The hooter of the old paddle steamer down the Clyde. The distant rumbling of waves on the coral reef, the background music of island life. The threatening roar of a gale, trees creaking, the wind hissing with the sand from torn up beaches, windows straining. Factory noise, never ending, forcing us to shout. The noises of bad housing in blocks with no insulation, cries, drains, lifts echoing up the stair well. An explosion, sound at its extreme where noise and pressure meet. The jumbo jet wallowing above the city with a following roar.

Voices angry, shouting, screaming; a chuckle, the smile in the voice; the orator who never needs a microphone; the voices with well-known wavelengths — Olivier, Gielgud, Churchill, Margaret Rutherford, Edith Evans, J.F. Kennedy, John Wayne and a host more; voices that frighten us with their coldness and sarcasm; voices that encourage us with the warmth of love.

And after the earthquake the still small voice...
Today if you will hear my voice, harden not your hearts.
For ears to hear, we thank the Lord.

Taste

Perhaps a more restricted circle of experience for most of us, though the gourmet and the wine expert may find here the window into happiness. But taste still means a lot to all of us, and the several meanings of the word remind us that what is good for one means nothing to another.

Fresh, ice-cold milk; a Cox's Orange Pippin; firm nobbly Brussels — as they call them in the market; a baked jacket potato with butter and salt; a small sweet tomato; the crisp part of lettuce where the green fades into translucent stalk; greengages halfway between green and yellow; thick marmalade; new crusty bread; passion fruit on ice cream; soup of all sorts; the well-done outside of the roast meat; poached eggs on toast; iced water on a tropical afternoon.

I imagine that is a very middle-aged list. Perhaps a younger list would start with chips, beefburgers, tomato sauce, chocolate ice cream and through to crisps of every shape and flavour. Do sherbet and liquorice still go together?

Then there are odd tastes which we meet more rarely. The chlorinated water in a swimming pool, the amalgam filling as you leave the dentist's chair, soluble aspirin and the sticky warmth of cough medicine.

Tastes which have shaken us out of our routine and which we don't care to remember — the taste of bitterness and defeat, the taste of vomit, the taste of fear.

Most of us are very conservative about taste, but gradually in Britain our cultural mixture enables us to meet the flavour of other parts of the world, and so we enjoy the sweet sour sauces, sweet corn soup, Peking duck, and — for some — the whole range of curries from India and Malaysia. We now venture into the cuisine of Italy and Scandinavia, the Persian Gulf and Hungary, so that France is no longer the only home of taste, though still supreme in cheese.

> The judgments of the Lord are sweeter also than
>   honey and the honeycomb.
> We thank the Lord for every good taste, and for the
>   goodness of the food itself not just on the tongue,
>   but for the whole of our bodies.
> O taste and see that the Lord is good.

Smell

How hard it is to remember, when we read historical novels, what a strong smelling place our towns used to be, reeking with sewage and horse manure, and thus how valuable were the pot pourri, the lavender water, the sachet in the linen box, the sweet smelling posy. Good smells were the only defence against bad smells. Today we expect less smell and are discreet with both sanitation and scent.

But elsewhere — travelling the Pacific Islands in small boats the two smells of copra and diesel oil were constant companions. Copra has a strong almost rancid smell, totally distinctive, which is the whiff of home to islanders who wander. Frangipani flowers, gathered on the grass, threaded on cotton to make garlands and put round your neck at every celebration, that is the sweet smell of the Pacific for me. Then the smell on opening up the umu, the earth oven, steam rising, the chicken and pork unwrapped from their leaves and their smell drifting towards the guests.

There are unforgettable smells in a hospital ward, in cordite, in slums, and there are distinctions between the slums of India and Britain, Manila and Naples, perhaps arising from the cooking and the laundry and the very stuff of which streets and huts are made. There are smells, apparently, in glue, though it seems strange that such an unlikely product should become an addiction. But with that there is the good smell of sawdust and wood shavings. There is a smell of incense, which goes back in history to the savour of the sacrifice, and lingers on in some Christian traditions.

And at home we know familiar smells — the encouraging smell of cooking when you feel hungry; furniture polish; soap; the first hyacinths, sweet peas and lily of the valley. Bonfire and fireworks. There is a series of childhood smells, from Bovril to dirty sports gear and the tang of acid in the lab. Industrial smells defeat us — windward of the tannery and you just suffer — but a bland talcum powder existence would perhaps make us poorer in the end.

A living sacrifice, may life and thought itself by be a
    sweet savour that is pleasure for our Heavenly Father.

Sight

Perhaps at birth this is the last of the windows onto the world that opens for us. Touch, sound, taste and smell go back further and in some creatures eyes do not open for days. Yet the very thought of existence without sight reminds us of all who are blind, just as our remembrance of sounds speaks of the handicap of deafness. To be without any of the senses is a tough obstacle, for we need them all. Our whole civilization is built on sight.

Colour. The greens of Spring in all their variety, from the ochre green of oak to the vivid green of beech and the delicate green haze of silver birch. The yellows of Spring, crocus and daffodil and forsythia and, so much more subdued, the primrose. Colours of Spring blossom on cherry, apple, japonica against the dark boughs and blue sky. Sea colours. Why is the sea so different in colour in different parts of the world? I thought it had a common formula, but what could be more distinct than the North Sea, hardly blue even on a good day, and the rolling seas of mid-Pacific? How subtle are the colours in light and shade, how they vibrate! And how different are the colours of industry from their natural origins — orange squash and oranges, tomato soup and actual tomatoes; fabrics, tapestry, stained glass, stone and colour wash, tiles; summer tan. Holly berries against their deep gloss leaves, the colours that shout Christmas. The beauty of black and brown skin and the whiteness of teeth in a grin.

Movement. Leaves shaking; the great fronds up there on the coconut palms swishing in the trade wind and the needles of the casuarina dancing in company. All the complex movement of clouds; sometimes with layers going in different directions. Movement in our streets. London buses and the distinct colours of Birmingham and Glasgow liveries and all the others that turn a city street into an action painting. The sight of young creatures playing. The stately dance of white cricketers against the green, and the dances of every nation in full costume. Movements of great skill, as when we watch the hands of a pianist, and movements that we do not have to learn, holding hands.

So we could go on with all the excitement and variety that comes through sight. But even so what we see is as in a mirror, dimly. We shall see the light and colour and glory face to face. I saw also the Lord, high, lifted up.

Lord God, how you have enriched our lives with all the pleasures of everything we touch and hear, smell and taste and see. How you have opened the world to us. Through our senses we know excitement and shock and pain and wonder. We feel with others, we are stirred, our anger is aroused. We are delighted and lost in joy.

So, Lord, we pray that our appreciation may not lead us into any false worship. Knock down our idols. Help us to look through the world of the senses, the world of measurements and the world of atoms to your creating power.

Thank you, Lord, for the imagination and vision and skill which you have given to every branch of the human family, for all great artists and designers who have enriched our societies, and for those occasional men and women of genius who have received something of your creative power beyond human explanation.

Hear our prayer for all who are handicapped and in one way or another grope in the dark. Help us to make up to them in love what they have lost in the senses. Help them to express what is in their hearts so that they may give to all those who think they can see.

TWELVE

Ecumenical Worship

It is one of the achievements of the ecumenical movement that, after seventy years of hesitant progress, no one any longer has to remark on the fact that worship is sometimes shared with other denominations. The amazing fact is that for so many centuries it was not so, that people who called themselves Christians should have regarded joint worship as a dangerous contamination of the soul, somehow destroying the purity of faith. There are still echoes of this in our hearts and we need to note them. But to rejoice in the measure of freedom we have is part of our prayer for ever greater sharing with others. For some of us this experience has been enriched by ecumenical conferences and training courses, special events; for others the key factor has been a regular coming together during the week of prayer for unity, or during Holy Week. Such ecumenical worship has much to teach us all.

First, we learn to dismiss prejudice as we face reality. It is generally true that prejudice feeds on ignorance. Those of us who air prejudice against our black fellow-citizens, for example ('Blacks never stick at a job' or 'Young black people are naturally violent') are not people who have ever truly known a black family. Similarly, Protestants who enjoy telling of the horrors of Roman worship have probably not experienced it as it has developed since Vatican II. We learn that robes and colours are not products of clerical vanity, but designed to speak of serious aspects of faith — although vanity remains a danger for all who lead public worship. On the other side there is probably far more thought-out structure in nonconformist worship than many Anglicans imagine. Since knowledge of each other is so valuable in dismissing prejudice, those who have a vested interest in prejudice, who are the extreme wings of most religious parties, naturally block the whole process. Extreme Protestants will never attend a Catholic mass and part of the reason for this is their fear that the experience will destroy their myths. I am thankful for the actual experiences which have helped me towards a more understanding view of other traditions.

Once we jump the hurdle of ancient prejudice we can begin to learn from the wealth of the great worship patterns. One of the major realities in our discovery is the wholeness and breadth which has sustained worship. Even a brief introduction to Orthodox worship shows us that the liturgy regularly presents, in summary, the whole Gospel narrative so that every communicant at the Lord's Table has been reminded of who this is who speaks through bread and wine. There is a wholeness of bible readings in many lectionaries, so that those who worship regularly hear all the New Testament and the Psalms every year with parts of the Old Testament also. There is a wholeness to the Christian year with its cycle of events which draws us to the key facts of the Gospel. Then within some of the traditions of the black-led churches we meet a wholeness of response to the Gospel, not only in the giving of an offertory, but in giving body, emotions and voice wholeheartedly to the praise of God. Such experience leads us to self-examination. We are asked to check on our own traditions to see whether we have presented the wholeness of the Gospel or just that part of it which currently impresses us as important.

Yet though we may enrich and enliven one another there are still difficulties in ecumenical worship. First, there are moments which jar on our sensitivities and we draw back, for example, when we join in Roman Catholic worship and hear the language of devotion about Mary. Perhaps we need to ask others what jars on them when they join our worship. I remember at the WCC Melbourne Conference there was a dramatic opening to each day's worship when a large cross was carried through the hall and up to the stage. An Orthodox priest told me that this was meaningless for him because we were seated and so not honouring the reality behind the sign. Second, we may sometimes attempt to bring together several traditions in one service, and this is generally not very successful, for the parts when wrenched out of the whole may no longer carry their original weight. For example, if the main order we are adopting has the major focus in the sermon, we cannot demote the sermon and keep the rest unchanged, hoping to achieve a more catholic emphasis. It is more likely that we can use some elements — hymns and prayers — from a variety of sources than that we can amalgamate traditions. Third, there is a problem about all the worship on major ecumenical occasions. It has to be written and printed. When there are several languages used and many people who are strangers to each other, then the written order becomes compulsory if everyone is to participate fully. But this means that the extempore element in worship is downgraded or even lost, to the impoverishment of the great ecumenical conferences.

Fourth, the major problem is, of course, the extent of sharing that is possible when the holy table is not open to all Christians. To hold united services which always exclude communion is bound to be a second best, and if we go on doing that for generations we may come to accept it as normal. To hold a communion service in an ecumenical setting and find that many folk cannot receive the elements is distressing and a goad to our conscience. I believe that we have to urge, and go on urging, the churches which have a closed table to re-examine their position. They generally hold the view that a total sharing of sacraments is only right if we have agreed on all matters of faith and order, then we shall come to the table as the crown on our recovered unity. I believe this is a wrong view. It assumes that all the members of the denomination are now united in all matters of faith and order, and that is most improbable. It assumes that differences in faith and order matters are grounds for denying communion whereas other human divergencies are no bar. It assumes that the denomination has the authority to bar any follower of Christ, as though the table belongs to the church and not to the Lord. I believe all three assumptions are wrong. The communion is for those who seek the Lord, those who stumble in the way, those who understand only a little of the faith and is not a prize offered by Christ to the perfect church. How better can we recover the unity of the church than by sharing together in that worship which most plainly incorporates us into Christ? There never will be an act of worship which carries precisely the same meaning for every participant, but there is already sufficiently widespread agreement about the purpose of the Eucharist for generous openness to be realistic.

Perhaps we might also think about one of the most teasing questions which arises beyond the limits of the churches — worship with those of other faiths. In multi-cultural Britain today we have to face this matter with great care, yet when we are invited to share in a multi-faith event we often do not have much time to think about our response. I expect that we would not, in any case, be unanimous about the response we should make.

Some will say that a multi-faith service of worship is an impossibility because, while we worship the God and Father of our Lord Jesus Christ, the Moslems and Hindu worshippers are praying to a different god, a god who is not God. Some would go further and suggest that we cannot pray with Jews, since they do not recognise in Jesus Christ the God of Abraham. A second area of criticism is that participation in inter-faith services creates a false concept of religion, a sort of supermarket approach, in which all varieties are offering equally acceptable brands of the same thing. Such a view is widely popular outside the churches. Very many people do see all the great religions as equally valid forms of the same inner reality, but those who are within a faith cannot take such an objective view. So we tend to reject two popular approaches. One is the philosophic view of comparative religion, that there are no ultimate differences between faiths. The other is the desire to worship together despite all the differences. Some would add the further point that the biblical call to worship does not rest upon the vague religious feelings of humanity but on the precise reality of thanksgiving to God for what he has done for us in Jesus Christ. Just as many passages in the Old Testament speak powerfully against the temptation to slip, drift, fall and sink into assimilation with idol worship, so the New Testament directs our praise and adoration exclusively to the One who is known to us in his

Son. to move outside that path is to depart from our Christian origins.

There is something that has to be said on the other side. The desire to worship is not a Christian monopoly. It is both wide and deep in the human spirit and is not to be despised by any of us. Some would argue that it is a primitive instinct which humanity is now growing out of, but that seems a highly speculative proposition beloved of sociologists who have rejected religious faith. On the contrary it seems to me that many of the most mature spirits of our age — in the arts and sciences, in medicine and law — still find the pull of worship in their hearts. If this is rejected by many today it is not equivalent to a new maturity, but to the pressures of a secularised society, and in fact is replaced by worship of secular objects. The desire to worship is part of us and is God-given not man-invented. So it is to be respected in every culture. We need, in this age, to ally ourselves with religious longing and hope, not to separate ourselves from it.

Perhaps an even stronger case is the reality of human solidarity in a nation and a world where this is a desperate need. The Christian duty, some would say, is no longer to separate ourselves, to emphasise differences, but to stress all that binds us with fellow human beings of other races and cultures. How can we contribute to the peace of Britain if we refuse to pray with those of goodwill in the other faiths?

Speculatively, but also worth considering, some would also suggest that Christianity, as we have known it, will actually develop into something else during this era of cultural mixing, so that a new world-embracing faith will emerge. We should not think that we are the end product of Christianity, or that the creeds define this faith for ever. Let us sit a bit more loosely to the language and concept of the bible and seek ways of knowing God that draw humanity together.

These arguments for and against inter-faith worship do not simply cancel each other out; they are, I believe, leading us towards a realistic and faithful position we can maintain. To me what is being said is that sharing with others in other faiths is now a vital matter for us all, for the peace of our society, for the discovery of a community and for Christian witness and pilgrimage. No longer can we follow Christ by shutting our eyes and ears to the entire religious experience of half the world. To recognise there a genuine searching for the deepest reality of life leads to human respect for each other. Such an attitude must replace the ludicrous caricatures of a former age when every Hindu practised Suttee and Thuggee and every Moslem wielded the sword of a holy war. Often the worst sort of xenophobia was imported into theology, and of that we must repent. But that does not clear the way for full inter-faith worship. The differences between the faiths are genuine, not imaginary. The promise of Jesus is to those who are gathered 'in my name' since it is through the name, character, life and spirit of Jesus that we worship. So while there is much we can offer to one another — our various scriptures, our common longings, our mutual repentance, our confidence in moral certainties, our united duty towards our country — there is not one full act of common worship which we can offer to God. We can listen to each other's worship, and that may be important to do. We can share silence together, in which each offers his own prayer. It may even be possible, when we have built sufficient trust, for us to expose our doubts and questions to each other and seek help. We may be given the opportunity of testifying to the reality of Christ. But to share in one common worship of God I see as only possible at the climax of history when we shall all be drawn into the worship of the Father of all and discover that Jesus Christ is for all the Way of holiness we have longed to find, the Truth about ourselves which we have studied to know and the Life in God's presence and power which both judges and fulfils our religious quests.

In the present, when difficult questions press on us, my plea is for generosity and hope. We believe there is one God, who is known to us in Jesus Christ, and no other. Therefore, if the prayers of people of other faiths reach God at all, then they reach the God we adore. Can we believe that such a God, who has a creative and loving purpose for each one, hears the prayers of Christians and is wholly deaf to the heartfelt longings of all others? We cannot here deal in proofs. But there is sufficient ground for sympathetic understanding, for generosity of attitude, for sharing as much as we can. For in such a sharing the wonder of Jesus Christ will not be hidden and we need have no fears for the universal calling of his cross.

Worship in the context of the world church is focussed for me by the Vancouver Assembly of the World Council of Churches. There the world church was made visible in a way that rarely happens, and the songs and prayers were in many languages from many sources. It was a rich experience of worship. A high point was a celebration of what is called the Lima Liturgy. This is a text developed from the work of the Faith and Order Commission over many years, approved at a meeting in Lima and issued along with the 'Baptism, Eucharist and Ministry' document. Here is a text with very wide acceptance among all Christian traditions. It does not overcome difficulties about ordination, which still prevent a full sharing in the communion. But it provides a basis for ecumenical services in future and is a further foretaste of the banquet to come.

Lord Jesus Christ, Who hast said that Thou art the Way, the Truth and the Life: we pray Thee suffer us not at any time to stray from Thee, who art the Way; nor ever to distrust Thy promises, who art the Truth; nor to rest in any other thing than Thee, who art the Life; for Thou hast taught us what to believe, what to do, what to hope, and wherein to rest.
(Erasmus)

Almighty God, whose glory the heavens are telling, the earth Thy power and the sea Thy might, and Whose greatness all Thy creatures that think and feel everywhere proclaim: to Thee belong all glory, honour, might, greatness and splendour, now and for ever, world without end.

(Liturgy of St James)

Remember, O Lord, Thy church, to deliver it from all evil and to perfect it in Thy love. Strengthen and preserve it by Thy Word and Sacraments. Enlarge its borders, that Thy Gospel may be preached to all nations; and gather the faithful from all the ends of the earth into the kingdom which Thou has prepared.   (Swedish Lutheran)

Thou art the Lord our God
In heaven and on earth,
and in the highest heaven of heavens.
Verily thou art the first
and thou art the last
and beside thee there is no God.
Gather them that hope for thee from the four corners
    of the earth.
Let all the inhabitants of the world perceive and know
That thou art God, thou alone,
Over all the kingdoms of the earth.
Our Father who art in heaven
Deal kindly with us for the sake of thy great name
by which we are called.

(Jewish Authorised Daily Prayer Book)

O Light! Creator of light, O heavenly Father, blessed art Thou by the ranks of the luminous ones. At the rising of the morning light shine forth upon our souls thy light of understanding.

O Light! Born of the light, righteous Sun, Son of the Father, Thy name is praised with the Father before the Sun. At the rising of the morning light, shine forth upon our souls Thy light of understanding.

O Light! Procession from the Father, source of goodness, Holy Spirit of God, the children of the church praise Thee together with the angels. At the rising of the morning light, shine forth upon our souls Thy light of understanding.

O Light! Divine and one indivisible Holy Trinity, we, born of the earth, glorify Thee always together with the heavenly hosts. At the rising of the morning light, shine forth upon our souls Thy light of understanding.

Let us glorify the Almighty God who made this morning light shine forth upon his creatures. May He make His abundant mercy shine forth upon them that glorify His name. Almighty Lord our God, save and have mercy.

(Armenian Orthodox Church)

Most great and glorious Lord God, accept my imperfect repentance, and send thy Spirit of adoption into my heart, that I may again be owned by Thee, call Thee Father, and share in the blessings of Thy children.

(John Wesley)

God almighty, eternal, righteous and merciful, give to us poor sinners to do for Thy sake all that we know of Thy will, and to will always what pleases Thee; so that inwardly purified, enlightened and kindled by the fire of the Holy Spirit, we may follow in the footprints of Thy well-beloved Son, our Lord Jesus Christ.

(St Francis of Assisi)

THIRTEEN

Shapes, sizes, heights and depths

It sometimes seems to me, as I visit many different churches, that the usual size of congregation today creates difficulties for worship. In a very small group, say less than thirty, there are great opportunities for informality and individual response. We can spend a time of conversation; the issues raised in worship can be discussed; in our intercessions each person can articulate special concerns. So the smallness of the group becomes an advantage. At the other end of the scale there are special qualities of worship in a large congregation when, say, over three hundred people come together. Then we find that a wide variety of music becomes possible, there are many gifts for poetry or drama or dance or painting, and the quality of preaching somehow becomes subtly different, for in the large congregation there will surely be those who find the personal message they need and the preacher can be confident that this is so. A crowd brings warmth, warmth moves into enthusiasm, and in that context challenge and promise are more clearly heard. Perhaps it is significant that the dynamic of the ministry of Jesus brought him the experience of teaching the very small group and the large crowd, but much more rarely the one or two hundred.

So I recognise a difficulty. Most congregations today are too large, and in too large a building, to attempt the intimacy of group worship, yet are far too small to generate the impact of a crowd. We thus run the risk of attempting the formal patterns that were developed in a period of great attendances yet in a sparsely occupied building, with the consequent dilemma of coldness. If we follow a prayer book service then this is not a major concern, for the pattern offered to us there is held to be of great value whatever the size of the gathering and in some cases there may be a legal obligation to follow it. I see some real values in this, for it does assure Christians that a full diet of worship is always available, not subject to the mood or inclination of the minister. Our non-conformist churches have not adopted this pattern, in order that the Spirit may guide those who offer worship to do so with local, immediate, pastoral and evangelical concern. How can we be faithful to the best things in our own tradition yet discovering new patterns that suit the size and shape of modern church life?

One answer that is adopted in a great many places is to vary the liturgy considerably over a month, so that, for example, there is a traditional communion service, a family service with work done by small groups, a service with a lot of music, several services with concentration on the sermon, and perhaps one that puts the emphasis on the healing ministry. The risk we run in such a pattern is uncertainty among the congregation. 'I thought it was going to be a proper service this Sunday, but instead the children were doing plays most of the time. Why can't we get back to a routine?' Or 'Is it that group with a guitar again?' Very good patient publicity is needed to overcome the inevitable dismay at the start of such a pattern. Another risk, which I think may be more serious in the long run, is that each type of service attracts its own clientele so that we find there are two or three different congregations which never meet. The fellowship of the local church is then in danger. One answer I met to this — and a surprising one — was in Holland, where a new church had been built on a polder site at the birth of a new town. It was shared by Dutch Reformed and Roman Catholic communities. The pastor and priest both led worship on Sunday morning with one early and one late service, but deliberately they mixed up the order. So the early congregation might have a Reformed service one Sunday and a Roman Catholic one the next. Not many congregations in Britain would be happy with such uncertainty but as an experiment it was clearly opening up great new possibilities for those with no traditional ties to a denomination. Perhaps more realistically we can arrange regular worship events which draw on the skills of both congregations. The problem of congregational divorce, however, remains a serious matter, even as regards the morning and evening congregations, which in some places seldom meet.

But there is a deeper and more hopeful response to our quest for worship models that enable us to praise the Lord in the situation of today. It is to go back to the main constituent elements and to ask how each may gather fresh power, represent our needs and confront us with the Gospel. One book I have found thought-provoking in this connection is 'Worship and Secular Man' by Raimondo Pannikar (Darton, Longman and Todd, 1973) which brings an Asian experience to bear on the modern separation of worship from life. He sets out the main rubrics or instructions that he considers are necessary as guides for modern worship — spontaneity, universality, concreteness (which together make up truthfulness) and continuity.

'Spontaneity' means our readiness to include in our worship whatever is most pressing in today's life. It is taking life with seriousness. So if we are caught up in quarrels it may be that true worship means dealing personally with the quarrel before we sing our praises to God. 'Universality' reminds us that worship reflects the 'all' of the gospels. As the cross is God's gift to all and as the Holy Spirit leads and blesses all believers, worship cannot be merely parochial, confined to a small circle of thought. By 'concreteness' Pannikar is pointing to actual precise signs as against intellectual generalisations. We do not talk and pray about giving unless we also handle money and place it on the table. So if we try to express the peace of God we give a physical sign of it to our neighbours. Then 'continuity' is a reminder that no order of worship starts from a blank sheet of paper but acknowledges the experience of the people of God through the ages. We are not divorced from our history, in which God has been speaking with his people.

To these I would add 'hopefulness'. Perhaps because of the decade since Pannikar was writing I sense a general loss of hope in the outcome of secularisation. Economic difficulty, repeated local wars, ever-increasing armaments, the frequent breakdown of marriages and many other signs lead many to adopt a philosophy of despair or total carelessness about the future. In such a society the essential Christian message of hope will need to be evident in our acts of worship, for a universal hope in Christ is the present message of the Gospel. Hope is now because acceptance and renewal in the Spirit is now.

If a congregation could examine its worship in the light of such criteria as these, then we might avoid that spiritual emptiness that arises from the repetition of generalities which have lost their force. The discussion could be very simple and practical. At what points in our worship do we mention today's concerns? How can we pray for personal worries and pains? What is there in our worship to remind us of the family of humanity? Are there features of ancient Christian worship which we still value? What is there in our regular diet of worship which binds us to all Christians? How does our worship affect daily life? These are not questions for the minister alone, or for the elders or deacons, but for the whole membership of the local church to consider, and they will be reflected also in the discussion of church assemblies. A discussion of this sort will help us to face the problems that arise with every size of congregation.

Two technical aspects of our response to such questions are to do with space and language. Public worship occupies the auditorium of our churches and central halls and cathedrals, so is affected by the shape and size of this space. When a new church building is erected today the architect seeks to form the space around the worship that will take place. But in most places we inherit buildings and find it difficult to adapt them, for the concepts of worship which they served in the eighteenth and nineteenth centuries are not quite ours today. There is one style which was very popular and still common in our own tradition — the four square meeting house with a gallery around three walls and a high pulpit on the fourth. Often the communion table in front of the pulpit was on a raised platform, with a railing around it. Acoustically this was a wonderful design and I do not know any better style for the preacher, for the congregation is near at hand, facing the pulpit as the focus and echoes are abolished by the breaking-up of the wall surfaces. In such a village church, perhaps in East Anglia, on a summer evening with low sunlight shining through windows on to the vase of flowers and the smell of hymn books mingling with that of cut hay, there is a warmth and intimacy in the church which encourages us all to open our hearts to God. And in the winter, when warm air rises from the steel gratings in the aisles, and the lights are dim under the gallery while light shines on the pulpit, the preacher is given wings. It may be theatrical and dangerous, but it works.

What we find so hard to cope with today is the rigidity of this form. The railed off communion table and high pulpit represent a hierarchical approach to God, so that when you are elected an elder you can go up one step towards holiness and when you are an ordained minister you can climb the steep ascent to heaven. The pulpit, the man preaching, is the undisputed focus. Sometimes the organ pipes take over, but the original design placed the preacher at the centre. Today the gallery often seems superfluous space, so that the height of the pulpit is a neck-stretching pain to those at the front of the ground floor, and the treasurer complains about the heating cost of all those cubic feet. Yet it is difficult to adapt such a cohesive design. The best developments I have seen removed the pulpit entirely and also some front pews, so that there was a large space available as a rostrum and on it a more modest pulpit, lectern and communion table in the centre. This allows greater flexibility of worship but, of course, has to be done with skill if the proportions of the interior are to remain in balance. We also have some excellent rebuilt interiors where a new floor has been inserted at the gallery level, the upper room becoming the sanctuary and the downstairs becoming a new hall.

Just as hard for us to adapt is the building with nave and choir, especially if the choir face inwards across the aisle and the pulpit is placed between choir and nave. This design which, with many offshoots and variations, comes to us from the medieval worship of abbeys with a resident group of monks, may be unhelpful in creating a sense of fellowship. It strings people out rather than bringing them together. The preacher has his back to some in order to face others. One variation that has helped in some places is to seat the choir in some part of the nave area, take out the choir pews and then re-arrange the space to provide more room for seats around the communion table. In this case, as in the previous one, the aim is to move away from separation to fellowship, a movement which is emphasised by our understanding of the activity of the Holy Spirit.

Yet fellowship is not just a crowd in a bus or in a bar or a football ground. The space for worship has to indicate not only that we are fellow disciples sharing in community activity but that we worship God who is always the beyond, the other, the stranger in our lives. In some modern multi-purpose buildings we find this is difficult. The very ordinary hall-type building, with a low ceiling leads us to expect a low-level conversation, horizontal in style. We ought not to blame the building, but simply note how our inner expectations are often formed by centuries of conformity with a particular style. Height leads our thoughts upward. That is the tradition, and it is not easy to escape, though there is no rational thinking behind it. So it is all the more important for those who plan modern accommodation, with the financial constraints that are normally present, to think through the other aspects which can help us to realise that this is not just a club premises — though it may also need to serve as that. Light, colour and texture come into play with fresh force and our skilled architects use them fluently.

This process of discovery, in which we search for fresh mixtures of the ordinary and the set-apart, also applies to the whole language of worship. I touched on this earlier in thinking about hymns and bible versions, but it is one of the continuing puzzles for the whole worship experience. How 'ordinary' can we be without becoming trite, how chatty and informal without losing the sense of the holiness of God? That sense was powerfully set out by Rudolph Otto in 'The Idea of the Holy' (first published in German 1917; English, Oxford University Press 1926) where he writes of the *mysterium tremendum*, that overwhelming otherness of God.

'It is in the light of, and with the background of, this numinous experience, with its mystery and its awe, its *mysterium tremendum* — that Christ's agony in the night of Gethsemane must be viewed, if we are to comprehend or realise at all in our own experience what the import of that agony was. What is the cause of this "sore amazement" and "heaviness", this soul shaken to its depths, "exceeding sorrowful even unto death", and this sweat that falls to the ground like great drops of blood? Can it be ordinary fear of death in the case of one who had had death before his eyes for weeks past and had just celebrated with clear intent his death-feast with his disciples? No, there is more here than fear or death; there is the awe of the creature before the *mysterium tremendum*, before the shuddering secret of the *numen*. And the old tales come back into our mind as strangely parallel, and, as it were, prophetically significant, the tales of Yahweh who waylaid Moses by night, and of Jacob who wrestled with God "until the breaking of the day". "He had power with God.... and prevailed", with the God of "Wrath and Fury", with the *numen*, which is yet itself *"My Father"*. In truth, even those who cannot recognise the Holy One of Israel elsewhere in the God of the Gospel, must at least discover Him here, if they have eyes to see at all.'

Now I am sure that many will point to the philosophical and social revolutions of the two generations since that was written, how the burdens of superstition have been lifted, how the threat of the black-bound bible has been removed, and man has come of age. But even when we acknowledge this considerable pendulum-swing in our patterns of thought, there still remains in all true worship a sense of distance — moral, psychical, spiritual — between the One whom we worship and ourselves. My concern here is that the modern language of worship, which has such great gains as regards our understanding and fellowship, may also be losing us the other basic dimension. Perhaps the modern exercise in liturgy is closest to the experience of Wordsworth and Coleridge as they released lyrical poetry from stilted forms and used everyday speech, at its worst becoming a nursery rhyme effect, but at its best timeless and reaching every heart. So we honour our modern writers of liturgy as they seek that vision and those words.

This is such a well-loved place that I hate to see it changed. Why must we pull out those old pews where my parents sat? Why do we need a cross up there? Why do we have a lectern when we used to have the bible read from the pulpit? Why....

O Lord, you are always God. From age to age we worship you for your love never changes. Help us to plan our church building so that more people may feel at home in it, free to praise you, and be at one with each other. Encourage us to look forward in hope and backwards in thankfulness and towards your kingdom here and now.

We are so tired of this old building. Never beautiful, it is now grubby beyond cleaning and weak at the joints. It smells of a victorian god. There is a darkness and heaviness about it which flattens us, makes us immobile and stilted. Could we not demolish it and start again?

God, our Father, you are always renewing what is old and wounded and tired. You re-make the light every morning and the year every spring. You bring new hope to those who are sad. So help us, in your Spirit, to enliven this church and make it a place of joy.

Thank you, heavenly Father, for all who have skills in planning our church buildings, for their understanding of how spirit and form help each other. May we have courage to plan for the future as we answer the needs of today, always expecting that the power of the cross will draw men and women to worship. May we value the presence of Christ with us more than any building, and the fellowship of your people more than the comfort of the sanctuary.

Almighty God....

Please stop a minute. What do you mean when you say 'Almighty'?

Simply that God is powerful over all creation, over all of us, over governments and over human plans.

But it doesn't seem like that to me. Nature goes on its way with no sign of God's power and our government certainly doesn't think about obeying God's will. Quite the reverse. It thinks of human power, not God's.

Well, you see, God is almighty but holds back his power in order that we may have freedom to develop and experiment and make mistakes, just like a parent with children.

Then 'almighty' must be the wrong word. No parent is almighty. As soon as a child is born the power of the parent is diminished, for the child has his own claims and rights and needs. As soon as creation began God ceased to be almighty and let the creation have some power of its own.

Yes, but God could still intervene if he wished. He could wind up creation today. That is what the reality of God means.

But you still have the wrong word. Suppose you said 'Humble God' or 'God of weakness' wouldn't that be more accurate language?

So the debates about language go on. All the words are inadequate, but we pray for such sensitivity in our choice of words that we my worship both in spirit and in truth.

FOURTEEN

A note on 'Given-ness'

One of the divisive questions that arise in church debate on liturgy is to what extent the worship of the church is an inheritance, given to us by the Lord and the apostles and the apostolic church, and not open to much change. Plainly there is an inheritance. We have only to browse through the Book of Common Prayer to recognise the wealth of devotional experience handed down to us. If we meet the Orthodox churches we find a living church which through the ages discovers in a set traditional form all the meaning and message of the Gospel.

I find it is not possible to go all the way with this understanding of worship, even though I am emotionally attracted by the fact of entering such a steadfast tradition. Is there then any 'given-ness' or is there a blank sheet on which each Christian community can write its own way of worship?

The given elements which I would need to hold to are baptism and Eucharist, as the sacraments commanded by the Lord; prayers to include thanksgiving and confession and hearing the word of forgiveness; the teaching of the people of God; and proclaiming the good news. Within the Eucharist I think most of us would accept as given the words of institution, the offering of the gifts, the prayer of thanksgiving, the invocation of the Holy Spirit, the breaking and sharing of bread, the sharing of the wine, the committal of all present to the life of faith. Such elements find their source in the New Testament and therefore cannot be readily dismissed or changed in any major way so that they become something other than the apostles gave to the infant church.

To go further than this and think of a whole order of worship as given is not necessary, nor, I think, helpful in the ultimate to the spirit of worship. To take as given the order of worship and most of its contents is to crystallise tradition at a point in history. It is saying, At that point we can see a right worship which is to stand for ever. But, of course, since that liturgy was written by people like ourselves, it was subject to human limitation of vision and the poverty of human words. It was shaped by a culture, and the culture was not all holy. Also if it was crystallised far back in the past it is likely that the particular liturgy was developed in one place without much knowledge of all the variants that were being used elsewhere. So it did not represent the worship of the whole church.

The process of development in liturgy has to be continuous simply because the human context changes. The meaning that carried popular assent at one period meets a blank stare at another. Retranslation is a constant necessity. But just updating words is never enough, for it is the emphases which also need to meet the human spirit in different contexts. Where people are downtrodden and treated like dirt, it is not helpful in conveying Christ to emphasise that men and women are but worms, or that they fall desperately short of the model of Christ or that their sins are like scarlet. A totally given liturgy assumes, falsely, that there is one perfect presentation of the faith which is right for everyone. If that exists we certainly have not yet found it!

Another problem about 'given-ness' in worship is that it restricts the creativity of the present generation while appreciating the gifts of people in the past. Certainly the saints of past ages did sometimes write like angels. Some of their prayers are classics and will be used everywhere. But I see no reason in our understanding of God and humanity to suggest that men and women today cannot write just as well. The great periods of upheaval in British Christianity — the sixteenth and seventeenth centuries — were times of liturgical development when the classical patterns of medieval Rome were subject to vigorous change. Perhaps the present century is also called to express, with powerful imagination, the fulness of the Gospel in fresh ways, and to say 'no' to such development would diminish us as disciples.

But the most weighty counterbalance to the very traditional emphasis in worship is surely our understanding of the Holy Spirit. Jesus did not write an order of worship for his disciples as far as we know, nor did the apostles write details of the liturgy for all the churches to follow. In 2 Corinthians Paul specifically writes of the contrast between old and new covenants. God, he writes, has qualified us to be 'ministers of a new covenant, not in a written code but in the Spirit; for the written code kills but the Spirit gives life.' (2 Cor. 3:6). It is evident that the freedom which was the consequence of this belief could descend to disorder. 1 Corinthians 11 and 14 make clear for us the very undignified excesses that could spoil worship. Yet the vigour of spiritual life was evident, drawing those who had found nothing but dead leaves under the trees of traditional temple worship. Where the church has deep confidence in the leading of the Spirit there is guidance for our prayers and preaching.

Shall we then move all the way to Pentecostalism or to Quaker worship and look at each Sunday as a clean sheet with nothing written there? I would not feel able to do so. There are given elements which I believe we have to maintain. There is also consideration for the life of a congregation which needs a steadiness in worship if all sensationalism is to be avoided. But the given-ness will, I believe, be seen in the broad outline of worship, not in the precise detail of words to be used at every point.

Before leaving this matter it is only proper to note the two most powerful arguments on the other side. A written, traditional litury is defended, first, on the ground that it is comprehensive and not subject to mood, whim or egotism. It can be carefully constructed so that all the major themes of doctrine are covered in a year, so that all the phases of prayer are met in each Sunday service, and thus all the needs of worshippers are, at some point, met. The second argument is catholicity. If there is one universal liturgy, then there are no foreigners at worship, everyone is at home.

Yes, but at home in what? To be at home in a text is not the vital matter of Christian faith — to be at home with people is far more important. The comfort of a known order is real, but is never the greatest good in worship. It so easily becomes a soporific. The mind switches off as the familair words continue.

Think how readily this happens even in using the Lord's Prayer. So I would fear that for myself the blessings of a prescribed liturgy would be overbalanced by the risk of a mechanical and, in the end, Pharisaic offering. I am ready to believe that other Christians find this is not so for themselves, but the risk is perhaps one that all of us should notice. Whichever way our worship develops there is always risk. Churches in the Reformed tradition risk the overpowering personality of a minister, a spasmodic reading of the bible and a lack of congregational involvement. We are reminded that God, who calls us to worship, 'has put his seal upon us and given us his Spirit in our hearts as a guarantee' (2 Cor. 1:22). He is, in fact, the only guarantee, for it is the Spirit, not the words, which God has given. Such 'given-ness' is risky but is wholly creative.

FIFTEEN

Purposes and Ends

There is this endless corridor with doors at regular intervals and I am bound to enter each one. Each door leads into a square room of identical size, decorated with the same paint, and the rule is that I have to stay in there one hour before I am released. Once inside the room — which has no view of the outside world — I have to sit quietly on a hard chair while above me, on the ceiling, the sprinkler system is turned on. For an hour it drenches me, but what it pours is not water but words. Who would not long to escape into the corridor where at least one can move?

This is a very dark parable which reflects the negative experiences of some who dread the regular worship of the churches but which does represent what some feel about it. Of course, it is not the whole picture; we shall look at the light parable in the final chapter. But I start here at this point in our thinking as a reminder that there are serious negative aspects to worship in every tradition, and you will spot some of them in the picture — the boxed-in feeling, the separation from the movement of life, the torrent of words, but above all the passive nature of the exercise. All you have to do is to sit under the valve and you'll get a soaking. Such passivity is all-too-much what the regular diet of worship encourages in the congregation, and from this we all suffer to some degree. Worship in the church is more exciting for the clergy who are operating the sprinkler and choosing the words. It is significant that this applies in most traditions and has been particularly true of non-conformist worship in the days of the 'great preacher', so we have a long way to go if we are to turn our doctrine of the laity, the people of God, into the regular Sunday experience.

Passivity — with it goes boredom and a static faith, the switched-off mind and the unwarmed heart. But what about the audience in a theatre when there is a great drama on the stage?

You may call that audience passive, for they are not acting, but they are deeply affected by the play. I think the point is that the stage play has to be a good play with skilled actors if it is to move our hearts, and the likelihood is that what moves us for a couple of hours will not affect our lives thereafter. The ordinary Sunday service never claims to be as theatrically effective as King Lear at Stratford. We have much less equipment, less time, and more diverse objectives. We are not putting on another persona but seeking to be ourselves. This means that to share in worship is not parallel to being an audience. What then are we there for, what is the purpose?

1. Purposes for the Worshipper

The first group of purposes can be listed as *assurance, comfort, forgiveness* and *healing*. Public worship establishes us in our faith and assures us that the lonely search of the human spirit for the goodness of God is not an individual quirk, to be played out in our private thoughts, but is the common pilgrimage of a great compny. We are, at that moment, offering the very intimate personal hope as part of the history of the faith. Today we sometimes decry comfort and assurance, fearing the smugness that can overtake those who are lapped in cotton wool. Yet I believe this remains a very proper element in our worship experience. God comforts his people. He offers healing to the torn mind and spirit, and for all those in our modern world who are desperately lonely, the company of the church is one form of God's healing gift. We all have, at some point, to meet the pressures and tensions of the spirit caused by death, when loneliness impinges and loss makes all life bereft of joy. Who can doubt that worship, in fellowship and prayer, brings the reality of God closer to us at these times? Forgiveness and healing have been primary purposes of worship from the earliest period of human existence and both are offered by Christ through the spirit to those who respond in faith Forgiveness, in the New Testament, is conditional. It is not the waving of a magician's wand which suddenly cleanses the congregation of all past sin; it is offered to all who humble themselves and turn away from sin towards the way of Christ, who share the spirit of forgiveness. 'As we forgive those who sin against us' is not an easy but a daunting formula representing a hard reality. So the approach in worship to the prayers of confession has to be full of realism, when we can genuinely consider our preparedness to enter the circle of forgiveness. Exaggerated language ('there is no health in us') may not help, but confidence in the gift of God is essential. I believe there is often a need for a period of silence during the confession part of our worship, so that we may each be ruthlessly personal.

The whole ministry of healing has become a topic of widespread interest and a wealth of books. In many places churches have sought to recover the ancient healing ministry which has generally been regarded as a sign of the power of the Holy Spirit. This has brought joy and peace to many. We are trying to escape from the notion of the 50's and 60's that a few individuals, with a special gift of healing, are the key practitioners who have to be invited to lead a healing service. We are coming to see the healing gift as part of the regular service of the church in which the whole fellowship shares. I believe we still have much to learn about the relation of physical ailments, physical ways of healing, mental and spiritual ailments and spiritual ways of healing. There are undoubtedly close links here which we do not understand very well. Therefore all of us who approach this aspect of worship will do so with careful thought about the effects. We do not live in the first century AD when methods of healing were often not far from barbarism, when the power of spirits was undisputed and the details of how the body works were quite unknown. So we take account of all that has happened since then as we have discovered more about how God's creation functions, and look at the scientific healers as allies, workers together with God, seeking the fulness of life for all. In our healing services we ask for God's blessing on the medical profession as well as seeking to relieve those who come in weakness seeking the strength of God. Just as we try to see the person as a whole, so we see the healing as a whole, and do not claim any exclusive powers.

This is all a purpose of worship to encourage, sustain, support and strengthen us. The second group of purposes might be listed as *learning, challenge* and *commitment*; these are purposes which break into our lives and prevent us from slipping into a careless, lazy, taken-for-granted religion. There is a lot we have to learn in our worship — the way to pray, the way to praise, the nature of the biblical witness, the character of a Christian fellowship, the application of ancient truths to modern life, and the ways in which the church witnesses to the risen Lord. None of this enters our lives without a learning process. Some may indeed be learnt as we study on our own, but for most of us the worship of the church is the major school throughout life. For this reason we probably need to give more attention to how we best learn, how words lodge in our minds so that we may feed on them in memory, and especially how we relate words to deeds, and the deeds of life to the words of worship.

That immediately brings us to the element of challenge. Every service of worship challenges us to examine the assumptions of our lives, to hold up the habits of home and work to the light of the Gospel to see their true colours. It is not, I think, the main purpose to criticise and condemn; we are not called to church each week to hear words of wrath as the staple diet. Who would rejoice to ascend the hill of the Lord if that were so? But the challenge is inevitable if we have ears to hear. The word of Christ in the Gospel challenges our notions of success, family, work, security, generosity, sacrifice, happiness and death. The more we understand, the tougher the challenges become, for the more vividly we discern the compromises of our lives. This is not masochism, but the experience we have of meeting the word of God in Christ; as we long to know the truth we also discover the pain of the truth.

When we learn of God and meet the challenge of the cross, we are led to commitment. For some Christians there is a single precious day of personal commitment which they treasure all their lives. For others, there is a whole series of events spread over years during which their response to Christ was formed. But for all there is a need to renew this commitment so that it is not forgotten or stale, moribund like the Latin learned at school. In some Christian traditions there are special moments for such renewal — in the Methodist Covenant Service, for example. In some, the sermon is very often directed towards an appeal for personal commitment. In others the regular Sunday Eucharist concludes with a prayer of dedication and commitment to the way of Christ. All are opportunities to respond to the Gospel so that we know more plainly who is our Lord and how we will give ourselves to his service.

The third major set of purposes can be called *praise, presence, wonder, incorporation*, all that set of mind and heart which acknowledges the glory of God and receives the grace of the Lord. It is just here that we often find ourselves in difficulty today because of the absence in us of any natural or inherited reverence for God. Secularisation has meant that the majority of our people grow up without any understanding of the word God, except in swearing. It is not a hallowed name. Yet public worship reminds us that we are in the presence of God who is the creative power behind the vastness of the universe and who yet is involved in the world. The enormity of the Christian claim, and the wonder of the word of God when it came to us in a life, leads us to praise and adoration. We are given a fresh view of the world — how small it is, how complex, how inter-related, how precious, how hopeful — so that the despair which pierces our hearts with the daily news is met with other news. At its best worship does not tell us a story but discloses a presence. It enables us to perceive the reality — which is always and everywhere a reality — that our lives are within the good purposes of God. As we saw earlier, worship is not the only way this understanding comes to us, but I believe it is the surest way.

As we are drawn to wonder and praise, so we are drawn into the new life which Christ offers. The significance of the Last Supper at the centre of Christian worship cannot be fully explained, but part of its meaning is certainly that we are joined to the life of Christ. He gives himself to us. He becomes one with us. We are made sharers of his life through faith. The eucharistic meal is certainly not the only means by which this happens, as we know from the experience of those groups which have a life of prayer and praise but no sacraments. It is, however, through the whole history of Christian experience, the most precious and catholic way of intimate personal sharing in the life of Christ. More than that, it is also an action of the community, so the worshipper is incorporated at that level into the body of Christ which is the church.

To re-instate this experience of awe, adoration and union with Christ is a very demanding challenge to all the churches in our chips and Coca Cola culture, in our computerised lives and enormously complex nations. It calls for all the gifts of art and music, the whole-hearted concentration of all who come to worship, and preparation in thoughtful prayer. To combine this with the intimate, the forthright, the everyday and the intellectually honest — that is the challenge to all who have these purposes of worship at heart.

2. Purposes for the World

Worship is not only directed towards those who attend a service of worship. The purposes, outlined above, might even appear to be a course of personal therapeutic treatment in which our pains and guilts are eased away, a massage of the soul. In order that we may never slip into such a psychology of worship it is good to remember that God calls us to worship, not only for our own sake, but for the sake of the whole society in which we live.

Public worship is a flag waved as a reminder to the whole of the community that there are truths and values and standards beyond those created by a consumer society. Church buildings are an ambivalent sign. They may indeed point towards a moral universe, but are just as likely to tell of an antiquated sect; they can bring a little architectural beauty into some dreary town, but frequently frown darkly at the world as a reminder of victorian heaviness and corpulence. In very poor surroundings they have been known to show that God is wealthy, which is hardly the Gospel message. So the worship that goes on inside the shell is the key reminder of what Christianity is, that it is all about ordinary people and their lives and the meeting with the Lord who speaks their language. Closed churches, locked churches, blank-faced churches give the wrong message. It is a lively group experience which is the signal that God, though as father-figure no longer part of every person's imagination, is now the creative power and ever-present judge and perfecter of all that thinks and laughs and loves and dies. Just as the apostolic experience at Pentecost carried conviction, so public worship tells its story.

Totalitarian regimes are suspicious of worship because it points so dramatically to authority above the state. In Eastern Europe this has been a constant tension for Christians. In Czechoslovakia I met Christian ministers who had to submit the text of each service in advance to the authorities. The appeal, so simple, to have a loudspeaker in the churchyard at a festival service was rejected. Worship was to be watched, regulated, censored because the state authority could not accept the public proclamation of a higher power. We have seen this struggle in Poland in recent years, and in Russia for a long time. A civil servant in Rhodesia said to me, 'How is it that when we see a country in the midst of civil war, the church is usually heavily involved?' The answer must be that when human rights are taken away, and when democratic processes no longer work, people discover in the life of the church a resonance, an assurance of the worth of each person and the hope of God for each one. So the value of worship in such societies is immense. It testifies to those realities which the dictator or party cannot control.

Worship is an invitation to faith. It says to the passer-by, 'Here you can discover a kind of truth that lasts for ever and a vision of what life can be.' I know that the invitation is often poorly expressed, with a stiff entrance to the church and a formal welcome and a strange liturgy. Sometimes the invitation is spoken by the sheer beauty of the cathedral close. Sometimes the village is drawn to worship by the gusto of the singing or the rhythm of the African drum. But in every human society the reality of doors open, a genuine welcome and a glimpse of the wonder of Christ is an evangelical witness which is to be maintained.

We believe that the purpose of worship goes far beyond the circle of those who are present. The prayers of the church are for the world. We believe in the activity of God in his world and in the effectiveness of the Spirit to awaken the human heart to fresh hope. So we pray for politicians, for the sick, for doctors, for the bereaved and for all sorts of human needs. We do this not out of obedience to a hard duty but rather out of care for the world, believing that the love of God finds expression in the human community. The prayers of others for us is a strengthening fact. As a young minister serving very much at the ends of the earth — when the map is viewed from Britain — I was conscious of the host of friends bound in a fellowship of prayer who were remembering the work and the people. We pray for others, believing that the blessing which they most need can be theirs through faith.

Worship, at its best, changes us and so invades the world. We are redirected very often by the word of God, so that we face the powers of this world in a fresh way. In South Africa today the experience of black and coloured congregations is that their times of worship enable them to cope with the harsh terms of life. The tragedy is that white congregations may say much the same, with worship as the assurance they need to maintain an impossible social system. It is because of this genuine clash of religious experience and conviction that the struggle in South Africa is of such concern to all Christians, who watch and pray for that justice which is our human reflection of God's equal love. Yet worship may still be the force which teaches and stirs us to action. Until it is translated into action it is incomplete. Work and prayer, in the old motto, were said to be so intertwined as to be one, but habitually we try to escape from this dimension to say prayers that we have no intention of acting out. Worship, giving God the glory and the praise, is the most powerful, steady instrument to change our attitudes and ambitions, and so to direct our social involvement, planning and politics.

The risk of passivity, the habit of sitting back and just soaking up the worship like blotting paper, is thus at odds with the purposes of worship. The whole experience is involving us at many levels — mind, spirit and body — so that the more we participate the more we shall discover. Every church service is an opportunity for a telling, rejoicing, healing, challenging moment for us all. Cold, passive, superficial worship is not worship of the living God. That is an old word which comes from Kierkegaard but which might be pinned up in our church porch today.

3. Purposes for God

Does God want worship for himself? You may think that we cannot even approach such a question. It is attempting to look into the heart of God, and that is beyond us. My reason for stating it is that I believe there is a theological danger in the assumption that God wants worship because he delights in praise. Like a king who needs flatterers to feel secure, so God wants thousands who bow down and sing of his glory. That is a very easy assumption to make and leads us into a wholly false concept of God. There are hints of this assumption in some of the Old Testament sermons on the jealous God who will not tolerate his people bowing down before any other object of worship.

I believe that a different approach brings us far closer to the truth. If we think of the world as the creation of God, then the fulfilment of that creation must be the longing of the Creator. How can creation be fulfilled? One answer is through the growth to maturity of every creature, so that the intention behind each is fully realised. Created and redeemed by God we cause God sorrow by our refusal to acknowledge both the source and the end of our life. We are not fulfilled, the purpose of God is incomplete, his outward action towards us finds a nil response. God surely wants our worship because in it he sees the response to his gifts, and that response belongs to life in the Kingdom of God. I have been helped to understand this in W.H. Vanstone's fine book, 'Love's Endeavour, Love's Expense' (Darton, Longman and Todd, 1977) where he writes:

'In the visible Church man is aspiring to create something which expresses his recognition of the love of God. His creativity is responsive: it aspires to be appropriate to that which it recognises. Since that which it recognises is love, it aspires to be a loving creativity — a kind of gift or offering. In the visible Church man aspires to make an offering to God; he brings something into being, or sustains something in being, as an offering to God, His offering is the symbol of responsive love.'

(p.106)

Worship is an offering, then, which replies to God's gift and says to God that we have recognised his gift of love and grace and hope. It is surely that kind of offering, made as fully and as freely as the Spirit enables us to do, that delights the One who gave us life.

PRAYER MOMENTS

Praise and thanksgiving

Thank you, Lord, for a new day and for our eyes to see it.
May we also see your glory in Christ.

God, I am amazed that your love extends to me. The better I
know myself the more surprised I am. Thank you for
such patience.

How would I live without friends? Thank you, Father, for all
who know me and care for me, with whom I can be
myself. Thank you for Jesus.

Our hearts and voices praise you, eternal God, because you
are beyond our sight but near to us, far beyond our
understanding but always with us.

To him who sits upon the throne and to the Lamb be blessing
and honour and glory and might for ever and ever.

We praise you, wonderful God, for the victory of Christ, for
his obedience in love, his faithfulness to death, and his
risen life for ever.

How amazing is the variety of nature! a million trees and all
different, ten million people and each one distinct.
Thank you, Lord, for the diversity of all living things.

Father, we are grateful for steadfastness. We value it in those
who are tempted to despair but never do, those who
sacrifice themselves and never complain, and in all who
stand firm for truth. Thank you for them all.

O Lord, how you share yourself with us in the communion
bread and wine. We praise you for this constant witness
to your love.

Laughter and tears and the shouts of children tell us of the
open heart. Thank you that, without shame, we can
share with you the private agonies that are hidden from
all others.

Thank you, Father, for light and colour; autumn leaves and
chestnuts, spring leaves, all the colours of summer and
the blue shadows on snow. When we see colour we
thank you, Father of light.

We are full of thankfulness for the gift of the Spirit. You come
in Spirit to challenge and teach us, to awaken
conscience, to lead us to Christ, to heal us and enable
us to speak the word of the cross. Thank you, Lord.

Urgent needs

Father, I am afraid. I cannot face this challenge. I want to
hide. Give me the strength I need for today, for I am still
your child.

This pain is overpowering and wears me out. May I have
peace and sleep and healing through the love of Christ.

One who is dear to me is in great trouble. Lord, I love my
friend, but you love more. May your care be made real,
may your love save today.

We meet to consider a big problem and the answer is beyond
us. So we seek wisdom and patience and the Kingdom
above all. Help us to see how your will is being done on
earth and may be done more fully.

Today we see the sights and hear the noise of war, although it
is far away. We are appalled by it. You are suffering too,
Father, as your creation is wounded. Teach us the ways
of peace. Teach the world the ways of peace, and help
us to be obedient.

What an unfair world it is, O Lord, where so many go hungry
every day. Help us to cherish the earth, to farm it well
and to share its produce with justice.

Today we have to vote in an election. We are not sure which
way to vote. Father, help us not to expect miracles from
politicians but to choose those with integrity, hope and
understanding that we may live in a good land.

Despair comes close to me, Father. Life seems so futile and in so many struggles I cannot win. Do you come close to despair? Give me a seed of hope. I pray this through the cross of Christ.

We do not know how to deal with violence around us. Theft and muggings, guns and bombs. Lord, help us to reach the hearts of violent people so that your word may change them. And help us to restore those who have been attacked. Grant us Shalom.

There is pain in separation, Lord. We are apart for so long and it is hard to remain at one. Bring us together again with joy.

Father, this dear one is leaving this life. But you are life and light for ever. I know we can trust you for the future. Keep this one in perfect peace today and always.

I can hardly believe it, Lord, that my marriage is broken. Was it my fault? Was I so blind? Help me to find your forgiveness and not to live for ever in the past.

Promises

Where two or three are gathered in my name, there am I in the midst. Help us to take this with seriousness. Challenge us with the marks of the nails in your hands and speak to us your word.

He who comes to me shall not hunger and he who believes in me shall never thirst. Enable us, good Lord, so to trust in Jesus Christ that our lives may be enriched by his presence for the glory of your kingdom.

He who believes in me, though he die, yet shall he live. May this promise be known in all Christian communities. The believer lives. The believing church lives, and death is not supreme.

When the Spirit of truth comes, he will guide you into all the truth. We need that guidance, Lord God, for we have only seen a little of the truth. Let us be open to all you seek to teach us.

Truly, truly I say to you, if you ask anything of the Father in my name, he will give it to you. We would ask in the name and spirit of Jesus for the day's needs and the world's salvation and the peace of God in our lives.

Behold, the Kingdom of God is in the midst of you. Open our eyes to see it, to see justice and self-sacrifice, courage and faith, freedom and forgiveness, and to praise you.

There is no man who has left house or wife or brothers or parents or children, for the sake of the Kingdom of God, who will not receive much more in this age, and in the age to come eternal life. Thank you for all who have so followed Jesus Christ.

Go...and behold I am with you always, to the close of the age. Your promise is sure, Lord Jesus. May we have the courage to obey your call and so to receive your promise.

Disasters

Today it seems a terrible world, Father, when nature goes mad and so many people die. Show us it is still your world where everyone co-operates to save life, and let us see your ruling and peace in the midst of chaos.

The doctor's words are frightening and I don't know how to respond. Must the person I love suffer so much? Lord, give healing faith, confidence in your presence, and no despair.

Our church fellowship, gracious God, is one of your gifts and now it is broken because a group has left in disagreement. We pray for the greatest gift of love by which fellowship may be restored and your name may be praised.

So now I'm out of work. Lord, don't let me feel sorry for myself but enable me to seek tasks that are worth doing even though they are very humble. Help me to expect blessings every day.

I'm defeated. Everything I tried to build has been knocked down, and my colleagues turned against me. May I have a glimpse of your reality — no permanent defeat, but always a glimmer of hope. I pray through the Lord on the cross.

Triumphs

What a splendid day you have given me, Lord, when everyone spoke well of me. Is that a danger? Yes, you warned about the inflated ego. Teach me that I am only a beginner in your school.

On a day when our country is victorious we remember all who cannot share the joy — the defeated, the sorrowing, the wounded — and we ask that our nation may always be magnanimous and not mean-spirited in days of victory.

That dispute was settled without war. May your name be praised. We say our Alleluia because your way of peace has triumphed over our way of violence.

The doctors have discovered a new cure. That is wonderful news, Lord, for your will is life in all its abundance. May this cure help those who need it most.

A new baby born and all is well. Heavenly Father, you are the source of life and love. Help us to receive this new life with joy and with carefulness. Lead us all in your way that this baby may find your salvation.

SIXTEEN

Vision and Reality

It was such an overwhelming feeling. I was there in the throne room of the palace, privileged to stand in such a place, overawed by the beauty, the gold and the lights, yet I was crying. For there the King was seeking to give us his message. He had the scroll there all ready, but it was tied up and sealed with heavy red seals. He longed to pass the message to us, and we were all dying to hear it, but it was closed, tied up, shut. The servants were all looking for a herald who could be called suitable to take the scroll and break the seals, a person — so it would have to be — whose whole character fitted the message, for when the King speaks the messenger has to carry the message in his heart. But as we waited there was no-one. Out of all that crowd of the wise and the beautiful and the rich no-one was fit.

Then, as I cried, I saw through my tears what looked like a lamb, just a white lamb, strangely marked with blood. But the face of the lamb was looking everywhere at once as though it had enough eyes to see all our thoughts. The lamb went up the steps to the throne and the King gave the scroll to this unexpected messenger. All of us in that great hall bowed down in absolute amazement for here was the one in all creation who reflected the heart of the King. The choir, which held the music and the prayers of all the saints of God, started chanting our praise, and it was music we had never heard before.

O Lamb, Lamb of God, you are the one, the only one
  to take the scroll and break the seals.
For when you were the victim, when your blood was spilt,
  you were bearing the pain and sorrow of us all.
You, Lamb of God, were gathering the flock, you called
  people of every language and nation and race,
And you set them free to stand here before the King,
  his priests and companions and children for ever.

Then, as the choir finished, the chant was taken up by thousands of voices, as though every voice since the first creation, every child, every animal, everyone in every language, was caught up in the same song:

Yes, he is worthy, the Lamb of God is worthy,
the Lamb who died is worthy
to receive all our power and wealth,
all our wisdom and might,
all our honour and glory and praise.

I did not think a greater song could be heard, but the crescendo went on. It was the combined choir of creation. All the fields and trees — where pagan worship once was held — all the mountains, all the clouds and winds that are signs of the spirit, the sun and moon and stars which we once worshipped, all were joining in the shout,

All praise and honour, glory and might to the King on
the throne and to the Lamb of God for ever and ever.

And as the thunder of that cry faded I heard the elders around the throne say, Amen, Amen, Lord God, so may it be.

(From Revelation, chapter 5).

It is a vision of worship in the heavenly kingdom, and perhaps a strained, difficult image for us, yet it is formed from elements which are central to our own experience. John was writing as one who had entered deeply into worship in the churches of Asia, or Turkey as we would call it, and who knew the struggles of small congregations in a hostile setting. So his vision from Patmos was not just a wild dream. It was in fact a very orderly account of the ecstasy that he saw in the presence of God.

It begins with God who has a message but no suitable messenger. All the ages were waiting for the word to come clearly, unmistakably from God to humanity, and in every place and every generation messengers spoke, but they could not convey the total word, just facets of it which had shone and were reflected like beams of light on their hearts. To convey the full message required not just a voice but a life. Only a life could carry the character of God. A philosophy or a logic could come in a book, a lovely form could come in a painting, but a Father's creating love required a creative life.

That life was found in the Lamb. It is a strange symbol for many human cultures where the lamb is unknown or known only as meat. Here it is the symbol of innocence and sacrifice, tenderness and acceptability to God. Jesus is seen not as King, the image so beloved by Victorian hymn-writers, not as general, not as the lion of Judah whose name was proclaimed, not as magician working miracles but as the unnoticed small animal which is taken from the flock for sacrifice. Here, says John, was that perfection of humility and obedience which perfectly reflected the heart of God, and so here was the messenger who opens the holy word to the world.

So worship begins. It starts with the choir, the crowd of believers who have come close to the throne. They are the ones who see the Lamb and recognise the meaning of the blood on him. They also are the ones who strain to hear the message and are in tears when no messenger is found. So they burst out singing with joy. Their song points to the Lamb of God and his redeeming death. But it is a redemption not of Israel itself on the old pattern, nor of isolated individuals for their private good, but a new saving action of God. He brings together people of every section of humanity to be a community with his own royal qualities, he lifts them up, so to speak, so that they are already within the Kingdom, partners with him in fulfilling the royal vision. Here John's glimpse of the purpose of God breaks out beyond all his personal experiences of the life of the church to see the end product. To him, probably an exile on Patmos, the fellowship of the church was small and powerless. It had not allied people with kingly rule but exposed them as victims to an empire's oppression. It had not brought universal fellowship but in fact was still, in his lifetime, an underworld activity in part of the Roman Empire. So he was seeing in the vision what it already was in the purpose and presence of God. It is an affirmation of the saving power of God's grace in Christ. It speaks of the realities of the Kingdom of God which are so often hidden from our practical, consumer-oriented sight.

But then, even more wonderful, the choir of the church is not alone. It is joined by the voices of all humanity, a vast number which can only be described as 'myriads of myriads and thousands of thousands'. We are led beyond the number of the actual church to the hoped-for, longed-for response of all to the Father of all. The church becomes just the prelude to the poem of praise, the overture to a great symphony. This at once provides a new perspective on what the church is doing and a new hope for the world of pain and sorrow. We see the church as the choir, that small part of humanity which can now sing the praise of Christ, but is there only to lead the whole body to a greater hymn. That hymn offers to Christ, the Lamb of God, all that the empire offered to Caesar. Power and wealth, wisdom and might, honour and glory and praise — a catalogue of what the patriotic Roman would sing about his King and actually see in the Caesar when he paraded with his army. Now, in the redeeming action of the Lamb of God, this glory is known to be wrongly offered to any emperor and is given to God alone.

Yet even that is not the end. The song of praise is taken up by the very material of God's creation. Just as there often seems to be a 'fall' of the natural world, a fracture or twist which allows perversion to attack the good purposes of the creator (who surely does not call the cancer cell 'good'), so the saving action has its fulfilment when every part of creation sings the same song of praise. Nature is not to be worshipped. It, too, is a worshipper. Jesus Christ as Lord really is Lord of all. So we look at the human body, the animal and plant creation, the elements, the atomic structure, the forces of motion and energy and light not simply as consumables. They are also our partners in praise. This is surely what Saint Francis had discovered when he sang of Sister Moon and Brother Fire. At this final moment of worship it is the elders or the choir who now say Amen to the universal song. Theirs is not a private in-group worship. It is not, as we have sometimes made it, esoteric but genuinely exoteric, belonging to the whole.

This vision of the great company of worshippers and their songs of praise is still a powerful word to all who now worship in what may appear to be a small scale. It speaks to us of the eternal Hallelujah in which we take our daily part. But this may still be too sweet, too idealised for our realities. So we look at the following chapter in Revelation and find there the hardest practicalities of all. For when the scroll is opened and the message is read, it speaks of the events which are ahead for humanity, sorrow and war and famine and disease, the very stuff of modern newspapers. It was the very stuff, also, of the experience of the early church. Theirs was no escapist existence, for earning a living, building a family, living peacefully with neighbours and avoiding an early death were the daily struggle for ordinary people. So the great song of praise is heard, in this climax of bible worship, behind and beyond and through all the events of human history. Sorrow does not blot out the song. Indeed it gives it meaning. For it is sorrow which wounds the Lamb. At the centre of all our worship, on earth and in heaven, is the Christ who enters into all our sorrow, who knows the sound of all our wars, who shares the experience of the hungry, and who calls us to be with him in the presence of the Father.

What shall I bring to worship?

Imagination — to see through stumbling words and old hymns towards the present reality of God.

Memory — because the past (both my own past and the history of the world) is not without signs of God's activity and love.

Attention — the mind loves to wander. At each point of a service I need to say, This is for me; I will listen.

Humility — to pray to God in recognition of what I am like, and how poorly I have represented Jesus Christ.

Courage — to hear the Word of God and know that the cost of discipleship may lead me to run away. I want to stay with Christ.

Humour — I hope to take the Gospel with utmost seriousness, but to have a lighthearted view of all the oddities in myself and others.

Expectation — Better things are still to come, more truth and light are to break forth, fresh strength will be offered and new vision shared.

O Lord, help me to come to worship trusting that you are the loving Father of all. I would know you more fully and follow your way which you have shown me in Jesus Christ. Yet so easily I hardly hear the words while my thoughts wander. I can look at the text and see only the difficulty of tomorrow's work. Impatience nags me. Lord, grant to me the spirit of worship so that I may rest on your promises in Christ Jesus and hear again your call and know that all I have and am are yours for ever.